THE UPS
AND
DOWNS
OF A GUNNER:
MY
LIFE
STORY

THE UPS AND DOWNS OF A GUNNER: MY LIFE STORY

By Albert Figg
(95 year old Normandy Veteran)

2016

Dedicated to my dear mother
(1878 – 1957)

Reveille Press is an imprint of
Tommies Guides Military Booksellers & Publishers

Gemini House
136–140 Old Shoreham Road
Brighton
BN3 7BD

www.tommiesguides.co.uk

First published in Great Britain by
Reveille Press 2016

For more information please visit
www.reveillepress.com

© 2016 XXXXX

A catalogue record for this book is available
from the British Library

All rights reserved. Apart from any use under UK copyright law no part of this publication may be reproduced, stored in a retrieval system, or transmitted, in any form or by any means, without prior written permission of the publisher, nor be otherwise circulated in any form of binding or cover other than that in which it is published and without a similar condition being
imposed on the subsequent publisher.

ISBN 978-1-tbc

Cover design by Reveille Press

Printed and bound in Great Britain

CONTENTS

Acknowledgements — 9

Foreword — 10

Introduction — 12

The Early Years. — 14

My Life at Chiseldon 1920 to 1929 — 15

Fernham, Uffington and Farringdon, Berkshire. — 31

1934 - 1939. Highworth, Roundhill and Crouch Cottage. — 42

The War Years — 53

The Battle For Hill 112. — 63

Operation Market Garden. — 80

Maas/Waal Canal — 85

The Anger — 99

Home to Married Life — 105

August 2011 — 194

Appendix 1 — 204

ACKNOWLEDGEMENTS

My grateful thanks to the following, who have supported me over the many years (There are so many, I'm not sure where to start. My apologies if I have left anyone out):

The first has to be my wonderful daughter, Annette, whose support has been something I have had, without any doubt.

Second, and it has been a very difficult decision to make, is, Simon Johnson. He has been the one that has stood by through my ups and downs, during the twenty years that I have known him. He is the person who, in 1998, helped me to find the tank, which is now on Hill 112, and encouraged the MVT to donate £1,500. Thank you dear Simon.

Third, are Michael Whitely and Family, who generously gave the infantryman statue to me free of charge, many thanks for that.

Many thanks also go to:
Ben Oosta, (Els Kantoorfficiency) Holland Tom Kelly of Bartlett Trees
Radio Mersey (Roger Phillips)
Rex Cadman, founder of the War & Peace Show
MPS MVT Martin Jones, who is one of the best cameraman in the business (top cameraman for the BBC)
Sean Heckford RBL Dubai for his support and donation
Lady Hawkins School.

And the many others from all over world, America, New Zealand, Australia, Sweden, and Belgium.

I thank you all from the bottom of my heart, for without all of you none of these project would have been carried out.

Albert Figg

FOREWORD

This is a remarkable story by this remarkable man.

Albert Figg gave fire support with his artillery field gun during operation Epsom and Jupiter, which was one of many attempts to dislodge the elite German Army and Wafer-SS divisions from Hill 112 and surrounding areas, during the fateful summer of 1944.

Hill 112 is, a gentle sloping hill on the Odon Valley under Caen, which dominated the entire Odon 'backdoor' around the heavily defended capital of Normandy. Beyond lay the big prize, the Falaise plains – 'tank-country' leaving the dense claustrophobic hedgerow of the Bocage behind, like a bad memory. But in the way were the best of the best the Nazis had to offer, elite Army and Waffen SS armoured divisions – seven of them at the height of the fighting.

Albert Figg did his very best to give fire support during the operations around the hill. But it was not enough for Albert; after the war, he returned and decided his comrades-in-arms of the 43rd Wessex Division should also get special recognition. Albert raised funds, and made sure a Churchill tank was put on the hill's 112 Memorial Site. It is called 'Albert Tank'.

After Holland, it was supporting Operation Market Garden, and then Germany, for Albert. How many people and generations to come did the Allied Forces and Albert help out?

At 90 years of age, he is raising funds yet again, this time to put 112 trees on the hill as a tribute to the fallen. More than 10,000 Allied soldiers fell during the battle for the hill - hence the name, the 'Verdun' of WW2, lest we forget.

On June the 5th, 2014, I witnessed Albert being awarded the Chevalier De La Legion d'Honneur, the highest decoration France can bestow upon an individual, befitting, at the Caen prefecture, the birthplace of William the Conqueror.

On July 12th we saw a remarkable ceremony on 'the Hill'; Albert and fellow veterans together with a British Army delegation and pupils

FOREWORD

Koen Van Parijs (Belgium 2014) A good friend of Albert's

from Lady Hawkins School marched past HRH Earl of Wessex. Afterwards, the famous French Vin-d'honneur was remembered as a warm, respectful occasion, where tribute was payed to the fallen-and to those who came back. I always fondly remember HRH the Earl of Wessex, turning around and coming back to say goodbye again to Albert (having almost forgotten when getting into his car to leave). This is how it should always be; noble is the man who helps out his fellow man.

For me, as a Belgium citizen, the Hill 112 ceremony, on July 12th, will be amongst the most precious memories of my life; I was granted the honour of wheeling Albert during the parade. Pride and gratitude do not begin to describe what I felt that day. Albert did his very best to help liberate us, and he hates it when I call him a hero (the hallmark of all true 'heroes'). After the war, he set out to pay tribute to his comrades-at-arms by writing this.

Albert inspires people to be thankful, to be respectful, to try, to try to do ones best, and to care. Albert is the man we would all like to be. He still does not like being called a hero.

INTRODUCTION

We have to have a starting point before we have the end.

My name is Albert Figg and this is my true story as I remember it. My father was Thomas Figg and my mother Minnie Dinah Figg [nee Streeter]. I was born on the 12th of June, 1920 and it was in the days when the wife worked all days and hours of the week. I would have been between eighteen months and two years old when I started to remember things that had happened. But it was when I was very much older that I told my mother that I remembered being carried up a ladder to my bedroom. It turned out that dad was building an extension and as he had removed the stairs he had to put a ladder up temporarily. My mum was really surprised and said that I could not possibly remember the ladders as I was only a baby. At this point I must mention that I was called 'babe' by my nine older brothers and sisters, right up until I was called up at the start of World War 2 in 1939 and how embarrassing that could be. However, back to the ladder; I knew I was right, despite my mother's insistence that I was much too young to remember this, but my sister Minnie, who was eight at the time, confirmed this when I met her many years later. Nearly all of my brothers and sisters had left home and gone to work. My older brothers Charlie, Jack, Tom, George and sisters Rose, Nellie and Minnie could, and did, leave school at the age of twelve. It was not until 1916 that the age was increased to fourteen by Act of Parliament.

My real life, as I like to put it, really started at the age of fourteen when I left school and started looking for work and also took an interest in girls, of which I had many. Yes, I was always interested in them until I was married in 1942.

It was not until 1996, when I retired, that I decided to write my life story, prompted by my wife Anne. She also encouraged me with many other projects I embarked upon. When I started writing, I began to realise my life was always about accepting a challenge from an early age. The more I looked back over the decades I began to appreciate that it was something I enjoyed. I also realised that I liked talking to people and asking questions, which most were glad to answer. Later on, after my wife had died, my daughter took over encouraging me to continue writing. She helped by typing up on the computer what I had already handwritten. The standard of my education in the nineteen twenties was very poor and my writing today is not much better. When computers came along, I was slow to catch on to them but I have since done so, which has helped my writing considerably. I can now make all the corrections myself, but I still have to get everything proofread just to be on the safe side, you never know what a keyboard can write all on its own!

I hope you will get as much pleasure in reading memoirs about my life so far, as I have in writing them.

Warmest regards
Albert Figg

THE EARLY YEARS.

I wrote these stories by hand in 1966, I am not sure when the computer came in to general use but I was a late developer and did not get to grips with a keyboard and mouse until 2005, just after my wife died. My daughter Annette and her sister in law Denise organized a two-month course with the Kent County Council Adult Education Centre in Faversham. My tutor felt that I needed another couple of months just to smooth off the rough edges. He said I was doing very well for my age and at the end he advised me to go to Sittingbourne for two advance courses.

[*Computer learning*]

It was during my second batch of courses when I attended the War & Peace Show and I was approached by BBC Radio Kent. They were broadcasting from the show, which is the largest gathering of military vehicles and their owners in Europe. The producer asked me if I could come and tell their audience all about my projects. At the very start, the presenter asked if I had seen myself on their website; this puzzled me, a web what? I'd not heard of such a thing, I hadn't been taught about the Internet on any of my courses. As I was to find out later, it was now up to me to start teaching myself about other aspects of computing. The presenter showed me the website they were referring to and there it was, 'Albert's mission'. I went back to finish the course and to investigate the 'Web'. Much to my surprise and delight I was awarded a certificate for my efforts as I had passed the course with flying colours at the age of 85! Who says you can't teach old dogs new tricks?

MY LIFE AT CHISELDON 1920 TO 1929

I was born in the last house at the bottom of Slipper Lane in 1920. My father was Thomas Figg, my mother Minnie (nee Streeter) and they came from West Chiltington, West Sussex.

There were 11 in the family, me being the youngest, the others being, Charlie, Michael, (Jack), Rose, Nellie, Tom, George, Minnie, Cissie (who died at an early age), Margaret, Dorothy and (Dolly)

[Mum and Dad]

I have so many happy memories of Chiseldon; Tipsy Toe Lane (also known as Gypsy Lane), Washbrook, where we use to paddle. The walks around Cow Hill with Dad, Mum and Dolly to the Plough pub, where we would sit outside with a packet of crisps and lemonade between the three of us on a Sunday summer's evening.

[*Margaret, Albert and Dorothy (Dolly)*]

The house that was home for us all those years ago is now beyond all recognition. I made a visit in 2009 and the owner kindly allowed me and my daughter Annette to look around. I knew it as a long house with a path running along the front. It had just one front door leading to the large kitchen and another room always known as the best room with the stairs going to the bedrooms. I can't remember how many bedrooms there were but I know mine overlooked the water well. The front room downstairs had Dad's desk, an incubator where chicks were hatched, and the room was only used on high days and holidays (Sundays). I always remember seeing little chicks in the incubator; it was a wonderful sight to see them hatch, breaking the eggshell, and then come out.

I do remember there was no back garden as the house was dug into the bank, so there were no trees or shrubs. On the right was a grass area opposite the front room, down the centre, a path, to the left a vegetable garden and at the end was the coal yard. There was also a stable, a pigsty and a chicken shed. To the left a bank led up to a field, where I used to play. I remember climbing up the bank, cutting the back of my leg on the barbed wire and falling down the bank, which was full of stinging nettles. My mother covered me with iodine and I looked like an Indian. Being so open, we could see Cow Hill from our door, and when we were playing there, mother use to stand in the yard and wave to us when it was time to come home. Our place was enclosed by a fence with double gates to the yard and a single four-foot gate leading to the house.

It was some time in 1918/19 that Dad gave up his job as a farm manager in Bishopstone and bought a house at Slipper Lane, Chiseldon. I have been unable to find out who he bought it from, how much it cost and how he managed to raise the money. Whether the coal business was part of it or whether dad started it afterwards I really don't know. Strangely, I know his solicitors were Lemon & Co, Swindon, who at the time of writing are still there. I have contacted them, but they say it is too long ago to help me. I would love to know.

As I've said, the first thing I can remember was when I was about eighteen months to two years old, being carried up a ladder to bed. I was told afterwards that dad was building an extension on the end of the house. It was to be a clothes washhouse with a copper to boil the clothes in and a toilet; this was a bucket under a seat, it being emptied each week and the contents buried in the garden. Mains sewerage was not laid on until 1924/5. All this work was carried out by Irish navvies,

I remember this being done. Mother did not like me going out to see them as their foreman use to swear a lot.

There is a little story – there are many more – but this one happened after the toilet was finished. Next to our house was a public footpath which went up to the post office and the Wesleyan Chapel, and behind the house was, I believe, allotments, and also a wooden shack where a man lived. I only knew him as Mark and he always wore dark clothes. What happened was, it was late one night, Mother walked down to the toilet, it was very dark and all she had was a candle and some matches – the candle often blew out before she got there. On this occasion she managed to get to the toilet but the candle blew out. Undeterred she got ready to sit down when somebody shouted out 'don't do it'. She ran out screaming and into the house shouting 'there is a man sitting on our toilet'. My brother went to see who was there and found Mark sitting on our toilet blind drunk. We have had a few laughs over the years.

Further up Slipper Lane from the house there was a footpath and next to it was a stone-built thatched house; It seems to have disappeared now, what a shame. It's the same with the Baker houses near the steps going to Cow Hill, I remember those steps being built. So many places have gone since I was there; the history of Chiseldon, it is called moving forward, what is going to be next, the old houses in Turnball? Come on the people of Chiseldon, stop this destruction of your heritage, sorry, but I do get very angry about things like this.

The thatched house, which has now disappeared, was occupied by Mrs Wright who had a very large dog – well it seemed so to me, but I was very young at the time, about two or three. I was running up and down the path in our garden when all of a sudden this dog jumped over the gate, knocked me down and then sat on me. I started screaming and Mum came running with a broom and drove it away. I have always been nervous of large dogs since. Another instance was when I was about three and somebody bought me some sherbert. You know what I mean, it was in a cardboard tube, wrapped in yellow paper, with a piece hollow liquorice that you had to bite the end off before being able to suck the sherbert through. When you'd finished the sherbert, you would eat the liquorice. Inside of the container you would find a little toy and in my case it was a small whistle. Inside this was a small wheel, which spun when you blew it, and it would make a whistling noise. Unfortunately, not only did I blow but I sucked as well and the wheel came out and went down my throat. All I remember was Mother pushing her fingers down my throat and pulling it out and then she fainted. Now, every time I see children putting things like that in their mouths I think of that whistle.

Carrying on up the lane there were houses on the left and what was a field on right is now a housing estate. In one house, about half way up, Mrs Cox lived. She was my schoolteacher at the infant school. She was a very kind and generous person and not long after the war I went back to Chiseldon and she was still living there. I'm not sure how old she was, but I would guess she must have been in her eighties. I knocked on her door and before I even spoke she said 'I know you. You're a Figg.' I'm sorry to say that was the last time I saw her. Near her lived Mr and Mrs Ash who had a daughter Betty and we use to play together, I think they moved away before we left.

On the right hand side of Slipper Lane and Tipsy Toe path was a pigsty. Opposite it was a farm [now houses]. I believe the farmer who owned it, a Mr Whatley, also owned the farm on Cow Hill. Further up the lane was a shop owned by Mr and Mrs. Miller, she was tall and Mr Miller, as I remember, was much shorter. She always wore black and was very strict but Mr Miller was just the opposite, I always tried to make sure he served me as he always gave extra sweets. I was going to school at the time – I must have been five or six – and my playmate, Alan Hope, had the idea of going into the toilet and having a smoke He used to supply the matches and I would get the orange paper that Jaffa oranges were wrapped in. It was easy to get it from the shop, but on one occasion I asked for cigarette paper, Mrs Miller heard me and asked who I wanted them for as she knew my brothers didn't smoke. About a week later we were caught smoking by our teacher, Mrs Cox. I think that Mrs Miller must have told her about me asking for the cigarette paper in the shop, so that was the end of that little episode.

Around the corner, on Turnball Road, was a bakery and cake shop. When you went inside, the smell of the cakes and bread was heaven, it made your mouth water. I'm unable to remember who owned it. Next to that was a row of cottages where the Archer's furniture makers lived. Winnie Archer was a friend of my sister Dolly's. Further down the road was snob shop, the boot and shoe repairer and again I'm unable to remember the cobbler's name. As you continued down you came to the Post Office. Mr Last owned that; I remember he was getting on in years, and if the weather was good, he would sit outside of the shop. I don't exactly remember, but it was either in a chair or wheelchair and he was always very cheerful. Now turn around, and on the other side of the road there was a row of cottages where one of my school friends lived, by the name of Hicks. I think his other name was Arthur but I'm not sure – the passage of time has taken its toll.

Opposite these cottages was a field that had a large number of derelict steam engines and old farm equipment in it. We had many happy hours playing on them – it's a housing estate now. Then you have got Mays Lane going up to meet New Road. My sister Rose lived in the first cottage, up some steps, when she got married. I am not sure about this but I believe there was a blacksmith in Turnball. We carry on around the corner and the Patrick Arms Pub is in front of you. Just before that, on the left, is the infant school where I went. Mr and Mrs Hope were the caretakers and lived there with their son Alan. I called on them after the war and the same happened as with Mrs Cox. I walked up the steps and Mr Hope came to the door and asked what I wanted. I mentioned that I went to school here and knew Alan. He called Mrs Hope and, before I could say anything, he said it's young Albert Figg, come on in and have a cup of tea and some Christmas pudding! It struck me as rather odd as this was in the middle of the summer! I shall never forget it. Mr and Mrs Hope were a lovely couple.

Across from the Patrick Arms was a shop where the owners had a parrot. They put it outside in a cage and it wolf-whistled at the girls and they would stop and look around to see who it was. It was very talented and when the bus stopped outside it would make the sound of the bell. The driver, if he did not know, would drive off leaving people standing. It also had a pretty good vocabulary of questionable words taught to it by the soldiers from the army camp; it could swear better than any man. The parrot also used to immitate the sound of a cat and dog, which was quite funny to us kids. We certainly learned a lot of new words and of course we were told off if we used them, but then, we didn't know what they meant.

There was a soldier's camp up at the end of Draycot Road, first built in 1914. (see David Bailey's excellence book The Story Of Chiseldon Camp ISBN 0-9534118-1-8

978-0-9534118-1-8 Chiseldon Local History Group).

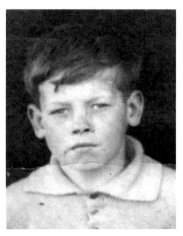

[*Albert aged six or seven*]

I had many school friends: Alan Hope, Bob Curnick, George Peck, Arthur Hicks, Betty Shellabeer and a brother and sister who were both deaf and dumb. Their names were Wiggens and they lived in Canny. I always made the effort to go and find them when they came home on holidays from deaf and dumb school. I could always make them understand. I met Betty some years after the war (WW2) and she showed me photos of the Chiseldon Carnival. This was held each year and it was the highlight of the year. My brothers used to decorate our horse and coal-cart and my sisters and I, together with other children, would ride on it around the village and then go to the playing field in Draycot Road, where all sorts of sports would be held. One that always fascinated me was push-ball. This used a ball about twice the height of a man, it was sponsored by The News Of The World and the idea was that there was a team of men divided into two that would go either side of the ball and push against each other to try to get it off the ground and underneath it to hold it in the air. Those who could hold it the longest time were the winners (that is how I remember it) and of course tug of war. This was usually between pub teams and troops from the camp. I also remember coal miners coming to the camp. I think it was either during the General Strike of 1926 or afterwards, they went to the Camp, which was then called AVTC (Army Vocational Training Centre) They also joined in the games, from my recollection and one actually died during the games.

Bear to the left and you go along New Road; there's not much there, only houses. Turn left into Mays Lane and ,if you go on further, the big house on the left (I'm unable to remember who lived there) is now a hotel, and a very good one according to my daughter. Next is the road to Canny, and then along you come to the turning back into Chiseldon. Down this road alongside the railway (which has been built on now) and past the field on your right was where Dad kept two cows, and where a circus was held every year. We had free tickets to it but it's housing now. If you carry on down past the houses, you come to the crossroads, opposite the Elm Tree Pub and opposite that, was the foundry. Further past the houses on the right and down at the bottom were Baker's cottages and the steps going up to Cow Hill and the church. Come back and turn left up the hill, with cottages on your left, and you'll see what was known to us kids as the big school. Mr Tatly was the headmaster. As infants we were always scared of him when seen, as he always looked very stern and we never saw him smile. I was not looking forward to going to the big school. Carry on up the road and you can turn right into Butts Road, leading to the cemetery, it was very scary at night in the dark and trees hung over the road. On the corner of Butts Road is a large house (I can't remember her name but an elderly lady lived there – more about her later). Turning left you go down to the church, the vicarage (with the Rev Waugh), past Whatley's Farm and then Cow Hill. There are some wonderful old houses there too. I hope they are all listed as historic buildings as it would be sacrilege to let them disappear.

Going back to the Elm Tree, and over the bridge, which is now demolished along with the railway, a victim of Beeching's reign of destruction of the railways in England. Turning right would take you to the station, and the goods yard. It was wonderful for us children, watching the big milk churns come in from the farms on horses and carts. There was one farmer who had a mule, a cross between a donkey and a horse, and that caused a lot of fun. If it decided not to move, it would not matter what you tried; several ideas were suggested but still it would not move. One idea, as I remember, was to light a piece of wood and put it under his tail, but I'm not sure if it was ever tried. The Churns were three-quarters the height of a man and he would lean it on one side, put his hand on the top, and push it round and round until he reached the place where it would have to stand ready to be delivered to London, Swindon, or wherever it was destined. Then he put it into milk bottles for delivery to the houses. Later, when I was fourteen or fifteen, I was a milk delivery boy, but in Highworth.

Let me return to my early days at Slipper Lane.

[*Brother Tom with the coal-cart*]

I started school when I was four and it was then that I started to understand more of what was happening around me. First the coal was brought up from the station yard on a horse and cart. My brother Tom, with the help of mum, put the coal into bags, loading them onto the cart and then Tom went out to deliver it. I was never allowed to get near the horse, cart or coal and the first time I was allowed to be on the cart was at the carnival, while I had my sisters and older children to keep an eye on me. As I got older, I was allowed to go and play with my friends. In those days one could wander almost anywhere for up to four hours at a time - being molested was unknown in those days. We would go birds nesting, but would only take one egg out of the nest, and if there was only one in we would wait until another was laid before taking it. I had quite a collection and we would pierce the two ends and blow the yoke out and then pack them in a box full of sawdust.

The other thing we enjoyed doing was walking along the railway line until we got to the golf course, and then going and finding snakes, killing them and hanging them up in the trees, I'm not sure why. From there we'd make our way to Coate Waters to the North. As the crow flies it would probably be just short of three miles from home, which to us was a great distance. It was unlikely that mother knew where we were – sometimes we would take sandwiches and a drink of orange with us, if we thought we were going to be out for the day. We were usually in a gang of four.

[*Brother Tom in uniform, 1925 (Somerset Light Infantry)*]

I saw very little of my dad during the nine years I was at Chiseldon, he was a bricklayer and very good I understand; he built the lime kiln at Ogbourne St George. I would like to know more about that. At a house or bungalow on the right going down Plough Hill, he sunk and built a well somewhere in Hodson, and he cycled everywhere. He also milked the cows twice a day so he was not a lazy man, but unfortunately he was a heavy drinker and spent most of the money in the Elm Tree, apparently coming home a little worse for wear. I was in bed when he went to work, and when he came home. This however left mum short of money and I was told later on by my sisters and brothers that there was many a time he gave her nothing. My brother, Tom, ran the coal business. He could only have been about fourteen as he was born around about 1907. That is what makes me think that dad started the business after he moved to Slipper Lane, no doubt to help keep the family as well as his drinking. He only paid Tom two shilling and sixpence a week. In 1925 Tom joined the army. Apparently there was a discrepancy in the amount of money received from customers and what was declared and dad found out. To protect Tom from a good hiding when dad came home, mum told him to go and sleep in the stable. When dad got home from the pub he found Tom wasn't there, but mum was. According to my brothers and sisters this was not unusual. Poor Mum, she tried to end it a couple of times but thankfully she was saved. It pains me to write this, however it was part of life.

George took over the coal delivering when he was only fifteen. Before that, he was working for the farmer, Mr Whatly. I was five then. I believed everything was going fine, although I was told later, that coal was selling for one shilling and sixpence per hundredweight for the best quality and just one shilling for second grade. Then, in 1926, the coalminers went on strike and stopped work. I will try and explain how this came about. Before, and after, WW1, if you did not work, you got no money. Women had no rights, no votes, and they were just servants, going out to work when they were twelve or thirteen, with most of them living in at their place of work. Mother was a butcher's assistant, but she lived at home so her money went to help the family. Her mother died at the age of thirty-nine and already had eleven children, which was normal. Some even had fifteen, as did one of my aunties. Mum's father was a rat-catcher and he used to like his drink.

In the 1920s a group of miners decided to form a union; this was a number of miners getting together and forming a committee and encouraging all the other miners to join. Their aim was to improve the wages paid to miners. It was dangerous and dirty work, and many men and boys were killed down the mines and their pay was a pittance. All the mines were owned by what were known as the Coal Barons, very wealthy people who were getting rich by the minute at the expense of the miners.

The government was mostly Liberals or Conservatives – wealthy people who had shares in the mines. It was against their interest to increase wages, so the union was declared illegal. However, the union carried on under cover until all of a sudden, in 1926, when the miners stopped work. The government thought that by letting the miners carry on without money or food they would end the strike, but no, it spread to the trains, so that no coal was being moved around the country, factories stopped, electricity stopped (although very few houses had it) and gas stopped. It then became known as the General Strike.

Eventually the government and the coal owners had to back down and pay the miners more, but the owners had their own back by cutting the amount of miners required to work in the pits. Their reasoning was that there was not enough room to store more coal and there was plenty in stock; there was uproar. The government decided that the surplus miners should be trained for other work such as farming, building etc. This is when the miners came to Chiseldon Camp. It was then that unions were allowed and the miners became known as the NUM (National Union of Miners). This followed other unions being formed, and many still exist today.

It was because of the NUM that the Labour Party was formed. The idea was to help the ordinary worker to have their say in how the country should be run (I'm not sure it has always worked). Now, the women wanted their right to vote, but they went about it in a different way. In World War One (WW1), the government called on women to work in factories etc. to make up for the men who had to go into the forces.

They also wanted married women as well, but this caused a problem as some had children, so they were encouraged to send the children to school at a early age. It was then that women started to get together. It was not a union as such, almost like the present day Mother's Union, and a Mrs Pankhurst was a leading figure in this. The idea was that they would encourage more women to work if the government promised to give women the vote after the war. When the war finished in 1918, the government of the day did not keep their promise, and so began the movement known as the Suffragettes.

Through Emilie Pankhurst, the organization gathered strength across the country whereby hundreds joined in disobedience to the government, police etc. They would chain themselves to anything they knew would hinder the government and police in doing their work. This persisted for quite a long time to the cheers of some people and to the annoyance of the men who thought that women should be seen and not heard and do as they was told. Eventually women got the vote.

I do remember, but not precisely when, a railway truck loaded with animal food came into Chiseldon station yard. Apparently dad and his drinking partners discussed the idea of opening the truck and liberating some of its contents as this would help feed their horses etc.. That night, they got their sacks, filled them up and away they went, but unknown to dad his sack had a hole in it, and as he made his way up the bank to the house it left a trail. The next day the police followed it and then arrested him. He was charged with theft and was sentenced to prison. I'm not sure where he went or for how long. As I have said before, I never saw him much, so I cannot say I missed him, but of course mother was getting no money. However, my brother, Charlie, who was working in London, sent some when he could. Some of the coal money was used, which in turn made it difficult to pay the coal supplier (Read & Son). During this period, the local council asked for prices from several local people with horse and carts to collect household rubbish, With the help of Charlie, George put in a bid and got the contract, but it took the council three months before the first payment was made, which did not help very much. It was then that Mother had to find something to do in order to keep food on the table.

First, she got a job cleaning the two chapels, Methodist and Wesleyan, every week. She then started to go out at night and sit with people who were dying, and lay them out ready for the funeral. That meant washing them and dressing them before them being placed into the coffin. The coffin was usually laid on the table where people could come and pay their respects. I remember going with Mother to an old lady's house in Turnball, before she died. She said to me to look after my mother, because you only ever have one. She died soon afterwards and Mum took me to see her in her coffin and told me touch her forehead and say God bless.

Next, two horses and a cart with two soldiers came to the house loaded with large bundles of dirty washing from officers at the camp. These were piled up along the path and mother had to wash it, starch the collars, and iron everything ready to be picked up the following Monday when another load would come. She would have to get up about five o'clock, get the water out of the well with a bucket. The bucket was tied to a rope and then let down. It was wound up using a handle which turned the roller that the rope went around. She then had to carry the heavy bucket to the copper pan and lift it up and tip it into the pan. She would have to do this about ten times. After that she would find some wood and light the fire to heat the water up. She would then call George, Minnie, Margaret and Dolly, the older children, and they would get breakfast ready before they called me. We would all get ready for school with Dolly looking after me, making sure I washed behind my ears and neck, something I always hated. In the meantime, Mum would go down to the yard and help George bag the coal and help him load it onto the cart. Goodness only knows how she kept this up, bless her. She was a wonderful mother, I know now why she tried to take her own life, and although I only found out many years afterwards, I never mentioned it to her and neither did I bring up the subject of Dad.

It was whilst she was sitting with a dying lady in the house on the corner of Butts Road that she collapsed and was rushed to Savernake Hospital with a burst duodenal ulcer. I remember going to see her lying in bed, looking very pale, but the thing that stands out in my mind is seeing a deer poking its head through the window. Savernake forest was full of them. This reminds me, every Sunday we would have to go to Sunday school, Methodist in the morning and Wesleyan in the afternoon. One of our treats, every year, was to go to Savernake Forest, take sandwiches, oranges, play games and look for wildlife; we had a great time. I have no idea why Dad insisted we go to Sunday school. He would not allow anyone to read a paper, do any washing of clothes, knitting, or sewing on Sundays. He himself never went to chapel or church, the pub was his only interest.

[Brother George]

It was 1926/7 and I was given the job of sitting on the back of the coal cart when George was delivering coal to the camp on Saturdays. This was because when George took a bag to one of the huts some of the troops used to steal another bag. The idea was that if I sat there I could watch and see it didn't happen. That was alright for a while, until the troops thought up a trick. What happened was that one soldier would come around the back of the cart and talk and give me some sweets. In that way, it took my attention away from the coal while another soldier would take a bag without me knowing. George found out what was going on and made me sit up in the front, looking down the cart, where I could see all the coal and what was going on. It was on one of those occasions, that I was sitting on the cart, when there was a tremendous noise coming from the air. It was during the time when people in black walked around with two boards hanging around their neck, one in front and one on their back, with words saying that the end of the world is near. Being young, I thought this was happening, and I cried, I wanted my mum, and as I sat there the noise got louder and louder. I then looked up and saw what look like a large silver object coming towards me. As it came over me I saw a big basket hanging underneath it and people waving. It turned out to be the R101 airship, apparently it was on its trial run. Unfortunately it crashed later on with a lot of casualties.

It was in 1927 that George decided he had enough with Dad and the wages he was getting. The council contract was proving successful and Dad had promised to pay him more, but he refused too. So off George went and joined the army. That left Dad with a problem, he had to get a man in to do the work that meant he had to pay more. It was not long before he found himself in financial difficulties. In 1929 he had to sell up. I was told he only had £50 left when we moved to Fernham near Farringdon in Berkshire, to work as a farm labourer.

There is one more story I must tell before we left Chiseldon. At the weekend, the workman would take the horse over Cow Hill to a field so it could graze. The workman would call mother to help him onto the horse's back to ride it. On this particular occasion the horse must have felt it wasn't fair, after working all week, to have to carry someone. When mother bent down to give him a leg up, the horse turned his head around and bit her bottom. She had a job to sit down for several days. My mother was such a kind, loving and generous person and she suffered so much, as did many other women; thank goodness times have changed. As much as I hate wars they have brought some change for the better.

The people I have strong memories of are the Rev. Waugh; he was kind, funny and very generous, he always had sweets in his pocket, and he use to hide some of them in holes in the walls, for us to find. As children we would always run after him to try and get to him before the others. He had an impediment which slowed him down and made our job of catching him that little bit easier. He often used to go and see my mother when people were dying so that she could go and sit with them. He always said to mum if her stockings were loose 'I see the cows have gone to grass.' I still don't understand what it meant.

The others were Ben Wellard, who had a withered arm, and also his brothers Eric and George Miller, who were all friends of my brothers.

FERNHAM, UFFINGTON AND FARRINGDON, BERKSHIRE.

In 1929 we moved to Fernham, near Farringdon. There was just Margaret, aged thirteen, Dolly, aged eleven and me, aged nine, plus Mum and Dad. Dad got a job as a farm labourer for a Mr Gilling. We lived in a large farmhouse surrounded by farm buildings with pigs and bullocks (which were cattle being fatten up for the butchers shops). The house and the surrounding farm buildings were known as South Farm. It is off the Fernham and Shellingford Road. We had to go down a long dirt track to get to it. It was situated in the middle of the fields, with no other houses around it (it is still there in 2008), unfortunately it has changed almost beyond recognition, like so many of the other old houses I once knew.

It was a wonderful place to be in with all the wildlife around us. The fields teemed with rabbits, hares, foxes and their cubs, weasels, stoats and all manner of birds. I must admit I used to get scared at night when you heard the foxes and owls calling. You could hear the rabbits squealing when caught by a stoat or weasel; many a time I would run out into the field to try and stop them from being killed or pick them up and take them home. Most of the time they finished up on the dinner table. We also had chickens so our table was never short of meat and eggs and our milk came from the main farm.

My mother really loved this place, and dad never went to the pub again. He used to play drafts with Dolly and dominoes with me, but he could not help cheating as he never liked to lose. If we complained he would just smile and carry on as if nothing happened. After a while we got used to it, but did not mind as long he was happy, which in turn kept Mum happy.

I never knew Dad to tell me off, or hit me, during all of my younger days. I suppose you could say I was spoilt, and of course I was growing up and was taking more notice of things. There is no doubt this was the happiest of my childhood and school days. The pleasure of roaming around the countryside finding birds nests in the hedges, skylarks singing, pewits (plover) in the grass. I used to pick blackberries, elderberries, dandelions and apples from the garden. Mum would use them to make jam and wine. Dad would drink most of it, though I admit I drank some as well.

Summer saw haymaking. I was taught to drive a horse and a hay rake, and how to rake the fields so that the loose hay could be gathered into lines and then picked up. Nothing was wasted in those days, and this is no doubt where I got the habit of saying to my children, 'waste not want not.' It is something that has stayed with me even to this today, all these years later, writing my memoirs. Harvesting was another thing I enjoyed. My job was to stand on the corner of the cornfield with a large stick to try and kill any rabbits trying to get away, but I never managed to get one. The corn was cut by what was known as a binder, drawn by two horses. This machine would cut the corn, tie it into a bundle, and then throw it out onto the ground. This, in turn, would be picked up and stood up, six at a time, into what was known as a stook. The stook would be there for two or three days before being taken, by horse and cart, to a storage barn ready for threshing in the winter. This was a very dirty job and something I always kept clear of.

I learned a lot about country life from the farmer's son, Raymond. We had to call him Master Ray, it was the norm in those days, and also touch our caps to Mr Gilling. He taught me how to catch rabbits with the use of ferrets and net the holes, and, when caught, how to kill them humanely, by giving them a swift chop with the hand behind the back of their neck. You had to be quick and firm so that they did not suffer and they would be dead in a matter of seconds. He also showed me how to pick up the ferrets without being bitten; they have very sharp teeth, which I found out on one or two occasions. The trick is that you have to get your hand firmly around their neck, as high up as possible, because they can turn their head very quickly and give you a nip, and if they fetch blood they will not let go. Raymond was killed when out hunting with the foxhounds. I think that the time I had at Fernham set me up for worldwide travelling, to see wildlife in its natural environment, after the war.

The school I went to was in Uffington, under the Vale of the White Horse and near the museum of the Tom Brown's school days book. We had a distance of two to three miles to walk, there and back, and none of us had bicycles then, only Dad. As I remember, we seemed to have much worse weather in those days than we have now (2008). Sometimes the snow was so bad that we had to leave school early; the snow was over 4ft deep on many an occasion. We took sandwiches for lunch, usually bread and cheese or jam and a piece of homemade cake. Mum was a good cook and could make a little go a long way, but I also remember her telling me, later on, that she had to go hungry herself many times so we could eat. How she'd done it I do not know, but we seemed to have a hot meal every night. I know she used to go to the farmhouse to clean it, and at Christmas she would pluck chickens for the butcher's shops. In the winter there was always a large wood and coal fire in our classroom where we would toast our bread and cheese; someone often brought a toasting fork to use, but if not we would make do with a piece of wood. Toast made in front of an open fire seemed to taste much better than toast made under the grill or in a toaster.

My teacher was a Miss Johnson. We called her Amy, behind her back, after the famous single aviator who broke numerous records for flying non-stop in the 1930s. She was the first to fly solo from England to Australia. She was killed when the plane she was flying crashed into the Thames Estuary in January 1941.

Miss Johnson was a real terror and frightened me nearly to death. She had a very short temper, but we got our own back because she had a gentleman friend who had a fish business and used a horse and cart to deliver the fish. If we were out playing, and he came past the school, we would call out 'Miss, your boyfriend is here'. That made her go red in the face, but then she took it out on us during lessons.

When I was eleven I moved up to the next class, which was the class run by the Headmaster, Mr Brinkworth. He wasn't much better and used to smell of drink. He was always passing wind, when he was near you, which was not very pleasant. We used to hold our noses, behind his back, so that others didn't think it was us. He used to ride a racing cycle and it was one of the boy's jobs, on Friday afternoons, to clean it, ready for him to ride home to Banbury, at the weekend. During the week he lodged in Woolstone near Uffington. I found out, after I had left school, that he was very fond of the school girls. Dolly told me that on one occasion she and a friend of hers were picked to go to the village hall and clean it, but it wasn't what they thought. Dolly told Mum about it but nothing was ever done; it was always believed that people in certain positions of society could do no wrong.

My sister, Margaret, left school at the end of 1939. She was the terror of my life, very surly, I never remember seeing her smiling, and as for arguing, where she was concerned, two and two made one. This was something that would annoy both Mum and Dad so much so that it was not long before she was packed off to work as a servant, I believe, but I'm not sure where. I do, however, remember her coming home on a racing cycle. Dad went mad, calling her all sorts of names, because she wore a dress when riding her bike, which was not very gentile, and would often reveal more than a young lady should. The next time she came home on her bike, she wore a pair of breeches. That did it, Dad went beserk and I don't remember seeing Margaret for several years afterwards. So then it was only Dolly and I going to school. We had made many friends in Fernham and Uffington including Charlie Pratt, George Watts and Charlie Webb (I understand he was in the Air Force during the war, and was shot down, but survived managing to parachute out, and then he was captured and shot). There was also Reg Baily, Jack Goodenough, Freddie Minns (who went down with the Royal Oak in 1939, when it was sunk at Scapa Flow in WW2). We were all very good school pals, but we can't forget the girls. One was Violet White who you could say was my school days sweetheart.

I met some of them several times after the war, but I would be some forty years older then. I used to find out where they were living and I'd knock on their door, but they wouldn't recognize me so I would play them on a little. I would ask them if I could come in for a cup of tea after all these years. Of course their answer would be 'why should I, I don't think I know you?' A few minutes later I told them who I was.

As I said, it was just Dolly and me now going to school, and it was my job to carry the satchel with our dinner in, but, as often with children, we did not always agree, and many a time I would throw the satchel down, and then Dolly would have to carry it. On one such occasion, I decided to try the smoking with the orange paper again and introduced the idea to my school friend, Charlie Pratt. Dolly found out and told mum; that did not improve my relationship with Dolly, however that did not last long and in most cases we got along very well. As years went by we became very close until she died 2007. The loss of Dolly really upset me. Dolly was in the same classroom as me; it was girls on one side and boys on the other. I was doing some writing - our pen was a pencil shaped piece of wood with a nib pushed into one end. To be able to write you would dip the nib into the ink, which was in an inkwell at the top of your desk. On one occasion, I put too much ink on my nib, and when I went to write, a big blob of ink dropped on to my paper. The headmaster saw it and he picked up the paper and wiped my face with it, Dolly saw him do it and she jumped up and called out at him in a loud voice 'you great big dirty pig'. Of course everybody laughed and the look on his face is something I have never forgotten. He first went red in the face, and then blue with anger, and then went out of the classroom to cool down. I think he'd had a couple of whiskeys, for he sat down and never said a word. He never did it again.

Dolly left school in 1932, we became very close to each other as the years went by. She lived with her husband, in Yarmouth, near their daughter June. Dolly had her eighty-ninth birthday in January 2007 and both Annette and I attended. It was a wonderful day with everybody laughing and joking. Unfortunately, it was the last time I saw her, because she died the following month. I can still see her laughing. Life can sometimes be so cruel.

It was then that the bond between Dad and me seemed to get stronger and also with Mum. I could never say anything against Dad, he was very good as a father to me. He even bought a cycle for me and put blocks on the pedals so that I could reach them, and taught me to ride with all the patience that that entails, much to the surprise of mother. He had a large kitchen garden and took great pride in it. He grew all of our vegetables. I remember going out there watching him hoeing between the vegetables, and planting, and for no reason at all hoeing between some cabbage. When he got home he asked me if I'd hoed his cabbage, and when I admitted it, mum looked at dad expecting to hear him to have have go at me. In fact he put his hand in his pocket and gave me two shillings (20p), Mum couldn't not believe it. I think from that day she forgave him for all his past. It was soon after that he gave mum some money to buy me my first long trousers. So there I was, on top of the world, riding to school on a cycle and in long trousers – that really put me at the top of the class with the other boys and girls.

I was picked for the school football and cricket teams. Unfortunately, we never had a proper playing field and had to make do with a farmers' field just outside of the school. We had to find our own boots, ball and shin pads, so we used paper rolled up and placed down in front of our socks to protect our shins. The teams we played were from nearby Standford in the Vale, where Pam Ayes was born. Her father used to come to the school and talk to us by the wall; he fancied a friend's sister, and mine as well, but he went abroad. I met him, years later, on many an occasion when he joined the Guards.

It was about this time that I started to take more notice of Mum's health. It appeared that the operation she had for a burst duodenal ulcer, when we were at Chiseldon, was not a hundred percent successful. One day, when coming home from school, I found mother in bed and being very sick, with tears running down her face. This went on for several years, and I used to dread coming home in case she was sick again. It was around this time that we had a lodger, Bill Toombs, who was a WW1 veteran. He was wounded in the head and at times he would fall down in a fit (epilepsy). He worked on the farm and he was a really friendly person doing anything he could to help mum. He brought a wireless with him, and, at this point, I would like to mention, that we had no electric, gas, wireless or television. All our light came from a paraffin lamp and we cooked in a coal-fired stove. Water was heated in kettles and saucepans and, once a week, a tin bath was put in front of the fire so we could be bathed.

Now back to Bill's wireless, which was known as a cat's-whisker crystal set. It had a wet battery, known as an accumulator, filled with distilled water and cells to provide the power for it to work. It would have to be charged with electricity, and this was done at one of many places where they had electricity and a charger. Two leads from the wireless would be attached to the accumulator, on the wireless there was a glass tube which was about 1in. diameter, and inside it was a very small crystal held in place by a clip. At the other end was a piece of very fine wire which was known as the cat's whisker, and attached to this, from the outside, was a small metal rod which you used to place the whisker on a certain spot on the crystal; you needed a very steady hand for this. Once you had done that, you then put the earphones on and listened until the sound was as loud as possible. There was also an aerial that went through the side of the window and was stretched between two poles outside. Only one person could hear it at a time, but Bill use to turn one earphone around so I could sit near him and hear it. If something interesting to Dad or Mum came on, he would place the ear phones in a basin (bowl) and the sound would echo The problem was that you had to be very careful when walking around, shutting doors etc. otherwise you would jar the whisker off its point. I was ten then, and it was the first time I had heard a wireless. I would also mention it wasn't until 1927 before I saw speaking picture at the cinema (Jackie Coogan) in Swindon.

It was about this time that I was given a Saturday morning job on the farm, cleaning out chicken coops and chopping firewood. I was eight to twelve and paid nine pennies in old money, (before decimalisation old money was twelve pennies to one shilling, twenty shillings to a pound). I saved this pocket money to help mum, Dolly, Margaret and myself to go to the Sunday school outing to Weymouth; it was the first time I had seen the sea.

I now have to admit to something unforgivable. Bill Toombs had been given a very valuable gold pocket watch by an army comrade he had saved whilst in action during WW1, he was very proud of it, and use to leave it by the side of his bed. He never took it out with him in case he lost it and I often looked at it, wishing it was mine. Unfortunately, temptation overtook me, and I took it to school and showed it to all my friends, making them believe it was mine. Sometime during the day I must have lost it, but never thought anymore about it until I got home. It was not long afterwards that there was a knock at the door, and standing there were two policemen asking Mum if Albert Figg lived here. She called me and said 'What have you been up to?' and it was then that they produced the watch and ask if it belong to me. Of course mum knew it belonged to Bill, but she could not believe I would do such a thing. I was very lucky as Bill forgave me and it was never mentioned again.

Another thing I use to look forward to was the Christmas pantomime in Oxford Theatre. The farmer, Mr Gilling, used to pay for all the workers' children and mothers to go – it was his Christmas present to us. Then there were the parties at school when the teachers seem to be human for once.

It was whilst at Fernham that I was taught how to milk cows by hand. This came in handy when I was in action in Normandy in 1944. There were always three cows left for me to milk when I came home from school. I was also taught how to get calves to drink milk from a bucket after being taken away from their mothers to be fattened up for market. To do this you would take a bucket of warm milk straight from the cow. You had to put one hand in the bucket with your fingers upright, and then push the calf's head down and put your fingers in its mouth. Your fingers would be like the teats of the cow and the calf would suck on them and draw the milk up at the same time. In a matter of a couple of days they could drink it without any help.

It was about this time that dad had to go into hospital as he had a lot of problems with his knee. He was in a lot of pain and he spent a lot of money on ointments etc. to try and ease it, but to no avail. The problem turned out to be what the doctor said was a foreign body between the joint; today we know it as arthritis which attacks the joints of the body. Together with that and the duodenal ulcer, it became known as the Figg problem. All the family suffered from one or the other; Dad suffered badly during his later years, but I remember him still looking after his garden in his seventies during the war. He would use two sticks, and when he got to the shed, pick up his fork and use it as one walking stick. Together he would dig the garden by pushing his stick in the ground and then dig with the fork, then he'd use his stick and fork to move to next piece of ground and start digging again. He wouldn't give in.

Nellie was the first to have the same problem soon after the war. She had numerous operations, but none proved successful, and in the end she had both knees muted. That meant that she had the knee joints removed so she had to walk with stiff legs. She used a Zimmer frame to walk, but of course sitting down was difficult. Margaret was the next to get it, and then Dolly; with both of them their knees became very swollen like a football. Dolly eventually had an operation on both knees, whereby she had metal joints put in to take the place of the worn out joints. I was the next to get struck down, and in 2000 I had one knee done the same way, and then, in 2005 I had my hip joint replaced. 2006 saw me have the other knee sorted and unfortunately neither knee operation has been completely successful, but at least I can walk with the help of a three-wheeled walker. Duodenal ulcers are the other family problem; Mother was the first, as I explained in my Chiseldon story and next was Charlie, the oldest of my brothers. Unfortunately he would not go to the doctor, all he would do was drink bisurated magnesia bicarbonate soda, which killed him in the end in 1954. Then George had it; he collapsed on the army parade ground in Devises in 1939 and was in intensive care for two weeks. He had an operation, but it wasn't successful, and he carried on in the army and reached the rank of Regimental Sergeant Major before being discharged as medically unfit. Tom was the next to have an operation for it, which this time was successful. He eventually moved to New Zealand where he died. Minnie and Rose were the lucky ones as they showed signs of it but only needed medication. I was the next, in the 1960s, when I was diagnosed as suffering from it. At first it was my wife who started questioning my bad temper and my lack of patience with the children, and me going to bed with stomach pains. In the 1970s I had my first operation, and then, one year after, I had another and although it cured it, I still have to have medication, and be careful of what I eat.

In 1927, Jack came back to England after eight years in the army. He served in the Royal Engineers (Signal Section) which eventually became the Royal Corps of Signals, and it wasn't until 1930 that I first met Jack. He married Bertha and was living in Rugby at the time. Joe Griffen, Rose's husband, hired a car and took us up there. He was working at the Marconi wireless station, where messages were sent all over the world, including sensitive ones from government offices. I think this is time for me to tell you about Jack and Charlie's work.

When Dad moved to Chiseldon, Charlie and Jack refused to go with him, as he had treated them very badly; they were made to milk the cows before going to school and then milk them again on their return. There were many more jobs at the weekend. Jack was always keen to learn, and he made friends with the vicar at Bishopstone who helped him to read and gave him books. When Dad found out, he destroyed them, saying he didn't need to fill his head with that rubbish, he only needed to get out there and work. In the meantime, the vicar taught him Morse code, which made Jack an obvious choice for the signals. He traveled all over the world with the army to Hong Kong, Singapore and then finished up on the North West Frontier between India and Afghanistan, guarding that frontier from incoming drugs.

It was whilst there in India that he set up an amateur wireless station (Radio Ham) in conjunction with the Telephone and Wireless Co.

They, in turn, set up a magazine all about the wireless and got Jack to write articles for it, including how to make your own set and use it. He turned out to be very popular all over India, and I had several letters sent to him from readers who wrote thanking him for his work. He was also one of the first to put a radio in an aircraft in India. When he came home he made our first radio, with a large, solid battery which you plugged into the wireless, and you did not require earphones to listen to it.

He moved from one radio station to another, and he eventually finished up in Portishead near Bristol, as a second/chief engineer. He set up his own amateur radio in his bedroom and kept in contact with all his old friends in India and around the world. It was whilst the war broke out in 1939, and as he was still on the reserve (army), that he was called up like Tom. It wasn't long before he was discharged and told to go back to Portishead and carry on with his job; apparently his work and his experience were too important to the war effort. This happened to quite a lot of men and women who were sent back to their jobs. Jack was also told to keep his radio receiver going. Very few people were allowed to do this as it was against the law in war time to receive or broadcast unless you had a license. He was to listen to enemy broadcasts, and whilst doing this, he heard that the Italian fleet was in Taranto Harbour; he passed the details on to the Ministry of Defense and the fleet was sunk.

He was also enrolled into MI5, and used go around the Avonmouth docks in the uniform of the Fleet Air Arm of the Royal Navy. He was telling me all this, much later after the war, although he was still under the Official Secrets Act, and I remember him telling me he was arrested several times, but released very quickly when he gave the police a number to ring. He was also in the Home Guard. I have two commendation certificates of his, which were quite a feat for a lad who was not allowed to learn by his father.

Charlie went to work as gardener at a children's home in London. He told me the story of how he got the job. Apparently, he got hold of an evening paper from a friend and found an advert asking for a gardener, so he applied, and got an invitation to an interview. Of course he'd had some tuition from dad, he told me that there were three waiting to be interviewed and he was the last to go in. He went to the toilet just to make sure he was the last, and then he sat near the door and could hear the questions being asked. So he had worked out all his answers before he went into the interview, and needless to say he got the job. It must be in the genes – I can see myself doing this – I had plenty of BS when I was in the Army and I know it helped me get promoted very quickly; no doubt those who read this and knew or know me will agree.

Tom came back to England in 1933, after serving abroad for seven years in the Somerset Light Infantry, and was placed on reserve, as were all ex-service men; they were the first to be called back to service when the war broke out. He married Evelyn King, when he was twenty-six and she was only seventeen or eighteen. He then worked as a farm labourer and was called up in June 1939 because of the possibility of war with Germany.

In 1934, aged fourteen, I left school, and it was not long afterwards that dad left the farm he was working on. He had a disagreement with the farmer, I think it was about his age as he was able to get his old age pension (sixty-five), and the farmer wanted to drop his wages. He was having none of it, so he got another job at a farm in Highworth, working for Mr Allen, who had a very volatile temper.

1934 - 1939.
HIGHWORTH, ROUNDHILL AND CROUCH COTTAGE.

It was now that I was beginning to feel my feet; I could stand up for myself at school with other kids, but now I was in a man's world. It didn't take me long to express my opinion, and it happened when we arrived at Roundhill Cottage, our new home. 'My goodness, I have seen pigs living in better places than this,' I shouted at dad, and told him what I thought of him. I can see mum standing there, with her eyes wide open, and as white as a ghost, waiting to see if dad was going to hit me. The strike never came, he just stood there looking at me in amazement, and then said that if he took me to heaven I wouldn't be satisfied. 'Not if it is like this,' was my reply. I then noticed that mum was smiling, as much as to say, 'Go on Albert give him what he deserves.'

The next day, he gave mum some money to buy wallpaper and paint. The cottage had no front garden or path to the door, and of course, as this place was in fields with no other houses around, the cows etc. could come right up to the door. Dad bought some fencing and put it around the house and laid a path to the door. I remember mother saying to me later on that it was the first time any of the children had ever told him off, they were always too scared. I have always felt a little guilty for making them spend the little money they had. I found out from Mum, much later, that he only had £50 from the sale from the house at Chiseldon, but at least he knew I wasn't going stand any nonsense from him to me or Mum.

Dad was working on this small farm hedge, cutting and laying, repairing fences, haymaking, building hayricks and then thatching them. He was a good all-rounder in farming, as well as in bricklaying. More importantly though, he was good as gold to Mum and me after leaving Chiseldon. By that time, I was the only one at home. The main farm, which was called Parsonage Farm, was in Highworth and was a mixed farm with cows, pigs, etc., but the main income was from milk produced by the dairy cattle.

It was now my turn to start working, and there was one place in Highworth where most of the people worked – the coconut mat factory. It was the type of floor-covering that most working families had on their floors in different colours. All the dust used to go through them onto the floor, so every week the mat would have to be taken up and the floor swept. It would only be the well off who could afford carpets as we see nowadays. I got a job there, but it only lasted a week, it wasn't for me all closed in. It was very hot and I was at everyone's beck and call. Dad didn't say a word and Mum said I was not to worry as something would turn up. Two of her brothers were gardeners, and the famous and popular gardening broadcaster was her cousin, Fred Streeter. Fred was Head Gardener at Petworth House in Sussex. I had the pleasure to meet him and his wife, many years later, at his house, in 1984. Unfortunately, they hadn't had any children, but they are in my family tree.

Back in Roundhill, the Co-op used to deliver our bread and provisions. Mum use to go up to Highworth by bus and get their pension and other things she would need. At this point, let me explain where our cottage was situated. It was just off the Swindon/Highworth/Letchlade Road, down the hill. On the right hand side of the road, there was a cart track and the house was at the end with farm buildings. To keep myself occupied, I went around with the Co-op deliveryman, helping him to deliver the bread, cakes and other groceries. He gave me a bit of pocket money, but also cakes and buns, and it helped mum, as in those days money was always a problem, but she never complained.

In 1935, Dad told me the farmer wanted to see me, and he offered me a job doing a milk round. I was shown what to do and who to deliver to. I had to learn to ride a three-wheel cycle, with a large box like container at the rear where the crates of milk were put in, which, when filled, was very heavy. If you have never ridden a three-wheeler, it is surprising just how difficult it is. When I first got on it, I thought 'this is going to be easy, three wheels, no trouble', but all I did was go round in circles. Eventually I mastered it. I had a book with the names of the people, but no addresses, so I had to learn and remember each house, and how much milk they had each day, morning and afternoon and enter it in the book. Sunday meant only one delivery, plus cream for those who had placed an order for it. I had to collect the empty bottles every day and to make sure there were enough for the next delivery. I collected the money every Saturday. It was a long working day, as I started six o'clock in the morning. By that time, the milk had been bottled by the dairymaid (who was the farmer's niece), and when I returned after the morning delivery, I had to light a fire under the boiler, which operated the sterilizer, so that I could sterilize the bottles. First, I had to wash the bottles using a long handled brush in a bath of hot water. When I'd finished, I had to stack them into the milk crates, load them into the sterilizing cabinet and then turn the steam on and leave them for at least six hours, ready for the next delivery.

It was several weeks after I started this milk delivery job that I had a flaming row with Fred Allen, the farmer. As I mentioned before, he had a heck of a temper, often shouting at his nieces and the farm workers, but not at me. I could not understand why nobody answered him back, but I suspected that they were afraid of losing their jobs. In those days, you could be sacked without a minute's notice. On this occasion, however, it was me who he was having a go at. It was all due to the fact that I had not collected enough empty bottles for the next days delivery, so I asked him for some new bottles which he had in store. Well, he went up in the air, screaming and swearing until he went red in the face and his glasses fell off, which of course made me laugh. This only added to the situation, and then I started to shout and swear back at him, just as he had done. Remember, I was only just fifteen at the time. The farmer, shouting and swearing at his workmen, reminded me of my father when we first arrived in Roundhill. I didn't intend to be spoken to like that, and although I was still a youngster, my view was, and still is, that nobody is better than me, and I am no better than them. So there we were, toe-to-toe, nose-to-nose, screaming abuse at each other. I would not back off and neither would he. By this time, the household, and some of the workers, were around us trying to stop me, but I was having none of it, and in the end I told him to stuff his job. His nieces managed to get him into the house to calm him down, but of course I was still going at it. One of his nieces came out and offered to get some new bottles, if I promised to stay on and to try and collect extra bottles the next day, but it was only when she promised to keep him away from me that I agreed. From that day on, I never had any problems with him and neither did the other workers.

In 1936, Fred Allen decided to sell the farm, and a lady from the North bought it. She was a lady in every sense of the word, and she was called Mrs Kate Hollis. She was married to the Director of the largest textile company in England, although he didn't come with her, but came on holidays. As well as being wealthy, she had two cars: a red

Bentley and a silver one. She had one son, called Gordon, and an adopted daughter called Mable. Mable was really good looking, with dark hair and dark eyes, and all the men in Highworth fancied their chances. She had a car of her own, a red two-seater sportscar, which made her even more attractive to the men. I found out much later, after the war, that she married the local butcher's son, Jack Reason, and as it was against the wishes of her adopted mother (Mrs Kate Hollis), she was disinherited. Mable died several years after the war.

One of the first things Mrs Hollis did was to turn the dairy farm into a Grade A farm. The farm was rebuilt along with a new dairy. She employed a dairymaid, who I remember was called Vera Cooper. She got rid of all the bottles and brought in cartons for the milk. Instead of the three-wheeled tricycle, she gave me a pony and a milk float, and that made my day. I loved that pony and named it Dolly. It got to know me and the area so well it would stop on its own at each house, and when I had made the delivery to one house it walked on to the next and stop without me saying anything. One of the perks I had with the help of the dairymaid was that she would make up extra pots of cream on Sundays; some customers had forgotten to order any, or friends had come to dinner unexpectedly. They were two shillings a pot and the extra money enabled me to buy a brand new cycle with three-speed gears. It cost £4/7s/6d. That's four pounds, seven shillings and six pence in old money, which is around £4.40 in new money.

It was at this time I was taking more interest in girls, and whilst on my rounds I saw a young girl also delivering milk from another farm. She was very pretty, but she was too shy to speak, so I had to find a way to get to know her. Her name was Eileen Figget. I found out she was only fourteen and still at school, but would be leaving very soon. She had a brother called Phillip and I decided the best thing to do was to make friends with Phillip, which I did in no time. It wasn't long before I was invited into his house and there I was being introduced to his mother and father, and of course to Eileen. I had now got my feet under the table, so it wasn't long before Eileen and I were meeting in secret. Unbeknown to Phillip and her father, when leaving the house I would slip a note into her hand saying where I would meet her and at what time. It was like a cat and mouse game and it went on for several months before her father caught us saying goodnight outside her gate. He had come out looking for her and when he realized it was me, he said 'don't stand out there, come on in'. We carried on seeing each other for a while, until another girl came along. This time it was Mary Braithwaite, the daughter of the farm foreman. She was sixteen, but experienced far beyond her age when it came to relationships… There was I at seventeen, having been brought up on a farm with animals and knowing a bit about what happens between males and females and the results. So it wasn't long before that relationship fell apart. That sort of thing wasn't for me, and it never was before I got married.

I was still friends with Eileen and her brother Phillip. It was during a conversation with Phillip that he mentioned he was seeing a girl whom I'd often fancied. I use to see her when I was delivering milk, on her way to catch the train to high school in Swindon. She would never speak to me. I always thought she felt she was better than me because she was still going to school at sixteen. I found out from Phillip that she was now working as a secretary at the local butcher shop, Reasons. I decided that I would take her away from Phillip; dog eat dog and all that… Within two weeks I had my first date with her. We went to the pictures in Swindon. Funnily enough, Phillip took it all in good spirits and our friendship continued. My friendship with Marjorie Woodward carried on with great seriousness, often meeting my mother and me with her mother and father. It was always thought that we would eventually get married.

It was the daily news about Germany; the Nazi Party and their war-like preparations were gripping the world. It was now 1937, and I often spoke about joining the army when I was old enough, but my brother George kept telling me not to do it, and to stop at home and look after mum and dad instead. It was around then my direction of life changed. I was ask by Mrs Hollins if I would like to become a gardener under her head gardener Joe Piner. I knew him and his sons very well. I spoke to mum about it, and she was thrilled as her brothers and her cousin were gardeners too.

Joe Piner taught me a lot about gardening, including how to look after plants in the greenhouse and how to tell if plants needed water by tapping the pots with a stick. If the pot made a ringing noise it needed water, if it was a dull sound then no water was needed. He taught me how to prune and thin vines, take cuttings and the most important job – cleaning the tools every day after use.

One of the jobs given to me was in the winter of 1937/8. Joe's words were 'I want you to plant some whips in the field opposite the house'. Of course, I laughed. The only whips I knew were the ones you used on horses. 'Albert', said Joe, 'the whips I'm talking about are small trees about eighteen inches high'. They had to be cut and heeled in; this is done by pushing the spade into the ground, pushing the handle forward, pushing the whip in behind the spade, taking the spade out, then pushing your heel against the soil and tree. It worked, the trees are still there and over 60ft high now. It gives me a feeling of pride when I see them.

My courtship with Marjorie carried on at a pace. During the winter months, one of my jobs was to make up the fire in the greenhouse every night for a week, alternating the weeks with Joe Piner. During my turn, Marjorie would come with me. It gave us the chance to be on our own in the boiler pit. This was about six feet deep with a ladder down to it. I had to arrange a couple of boxes in the pit to sit on near the fire, so we could talk of our future, and of course have a kiss and a cuddle... Mrs Hollis caught us one night. She looked in and said, with a smile on her face, 'Don't forget to turn out the light when you go, Albert'. She was brilliant and very understanding. After that she would let us have the use of her paddle-boat at Letchlade on the Thames. It was only three miles from where I lived, a very easy cycle ride. The Thames was a favourite on a Sunday. As with all places it has changed a lot. I took Annette, my daughter, there in 2008 and she could see why we always went there.

In 1938, Mr Neville Chamberlain, the Prime Minister, made the historic journey to Germany to meet Adolf Hitler and to get him to agree to a peace proposal to halt any war-like action he may be planning. Chamberlain returned, famously waving a piece of paper saying we have peace in our time. Nobody believed it and preparations for war started, but only in a modest way. I noticed a large factory was being built along the road I took going into Swindon (South Marston), and there was also a new railway cutting going under the road into the site. It eventually turned out to be an aircraft factory making Spitfires. They had also built a landing strip alongside it. The site is now the Honda car factory and industrial site.

It was about this time Mrs Hollis required our cottage for her shepherd, Jim Chester. His son and I became very good friends, as he was the same age as me. Mrs Hollis rented another cottage from Fred Gee just up the Letchlade Road on Crouch Lane, it was Crouch Farm and at that time it was a triple cottage but it was turned into a semi-detached property after the war. We had the middle cottage. Next door to us was a Mr and Mrs Lowe with two daughters, and he had a small holding rented from the local council. It was after the First World War that the Government made a grant available to councils to buy agricultural land and rent it out to troops who had knowledge of farming. However, this was taken away from him during the second war by the Ministry of Agriculture and given to Fred Gee, as it was not viable for one person to run every acre of land. It was subject to MoA, inspection and farmers were told what they should grow; the country had to be self-sufficient. Kitchen gardens, parks and even playing fields were all used to boost production. Vegetables were about the only things that were not rationed during the war.

1938 carried on in a normal way, although I was taking more notice of what was going on in Germany. News came through of atrocities being carried out against the Jews by the Nazis; we thought it could not possibly be true. We could not have been more wrong. There were Jewish shops being burnt to the ground, concentration camps, gas chambers, and forced labour.

The next big news was that the German Army was on the move, first crossing the Rhine and taking back land which was given to the French after WW1 to try and protect France from any future attacks from Germany. From there they marched into Austria, saying the country rightly belonged to Germany. The letter brought back from Germany by Chamberlain was now in tatters. Winston Churchill MP had been warning the British government since Hitler came to power in the early 1930s that Germany was preparing for war, but very few had listened to him.

Churchill had very secret information which could have only come from a member of the Cabinet. Apparently he had a friend in the Government who was also concerned about Germany's intentions. Churchill started to ask questions in parliament, which caused an uproar and led to Churchill being ridiculed as a warmonger. Time proved him right.

Christmas came and went and then things started to happen. First of all large aircraft, appeared overhead. Now that scared me. I had never seen such sinister-looking things before; they looked enormous, with two large engines. It turned out to be a morale booster to try and convince the public that we were ready for war if it came. Long deep trenches were being dug in London's parks to shelter people from bomb blasts. Concrete shelters were being built all over the country. Gas masks were being issued and arrangements being made to evacuate children from the cities to the countryside to protect them from possible air raids.

In February the Ministry of Defence started to ask for volunteers to join the Forces. It was then my friends suggested that I should join the Territorial Army, in particular the Royal Artillery, 112 Field Regiment in Swindon. I knew at some time or other I would be called up, and would have to go wherever I was sent. My friend also pointed out to me not to join the Infantry, as the chances of getting killed were greater than being in the Artillery. Being killed was something that was never in my mind, even when I was in action. In the Artillery you were at least three miles behind the front line. (We got called the nickname of 'Five Mile Snipers' by the Infantry). I joined the Artillery. Fortunately, mum and dad understood.

They both knew what war was all about as they had seen the First World War; both mum and dad had lost brothers in it. But to me, being only eighteen in 1939, the war seemed exciting. I was nineteen on the twelfth of June. I don't think any of us at that age had any idea of what was to come, but it soon hit home when we saw the lists of names of those killed in the papers, amounting to hundreds each day.

[*Albert in uniform with friend, 1939*]

We were issued uniforms with brass-buttoned tunics, a peaked cap and other equipment including a haversack, water bottles and an overcoat, but no small arms. There was always a shortage of weapons and ammunition. The government always had a very high priority for financing the defence of the country. To give you an example, my regiment had only two 4.5 Howitzers when we should have had 24, and we had no vehicles with which to tow them. We had to hire local flatbed lorries when we went out on exercise once a month at weekends. We had to take our own food, and light our own fires to boil our water. We had a cook but he was there to serve the officers only.

Twice a week in the evenings on a Tuesday and Thursday, I rode the twelve mile round trip to the drill hall at Prospect Hill in old town Swindon. There I was taught how to stand to attention, salute, slope arms, present arms; all with a broomstick standing in for a rifle. I was lucky in this department, in so far as my brother George had taught me when he was on leave. I was about eight then, and use to practice marching up and down the garden path shouting orders to myself.

'Left right, left right, left right', I would shout to myself. Mum used to stand at the door laughing. By the end of about two weeks I was top of my section and I was now allowed to go on the guns. We had to start by learning how they worked; after all, that's what I joined the artillery for, and my goal was to become a sergeant.

In June 1939, the regiment went on the yearly camp to the live firing range. It was two weeks at Oakhampton in Cornwall. It was compulsory for all employers of Territorial Army men to release us to attend, on full wages. All TA members were also paid two pounds per year. Going away was something new to me, especially with so many men. We slept in barracks with twenty to a room. We had bunk beds, and because I was one of the new recruits I had to sleep on the top bunk.

As I had been training on the guns at the drill hall, I thought I would be included in the gun crew on the firing range, but I wasn't, and I had to learn the hard way. The first week I was on cookhouse fatigues, peeling spuds, cleaning the mess room and helping the cook. The second week I was cleaning the toilets, and helping to clean the guns after they were returned from the firing range. That was my two weeks' training. That however did not put me off. I remember saying to my brother George that I would be a sergeant in two years, at the age of twenty-two… And I did it.

Now back to work in the gardens, and of course with Marjorie. The news of war was looking ominous. Hitler was now demanding that that Poland should hand back the ground that was taken from them after WW1, which was called the Danzig Corridor. As a result of the threat to Poland by the Germans, the French and British Governments of the day signed a pact that if the Germans invaded Poland, they would come to the country's aid.

It was on the first day of September in 1939 that a message came over the radio from the Prime Minister, saying that Germany had invaded Poland and that he had given Germany an ultimatum to withdraw her troops by 11 o'clock on Sunday the 3rd of September, and that if they did not comply we would declare war on Germany. At the same time it was announced that all Territorials should report to their drill halls and be prepared to be mobilized for active service.

After more than 70 years, I still remember it well. I know it sounds stupid, but I was so excited about the prospect of war. We were very young then, and we wanted to be involved with anything that was new. When Mary, the maid of the house, told me I had to go and report to my Regimental drill hall, I finished the lawn that I was mowing in record time. The mower had never moved so fast in its life. I took the mower back to the shed and I remember Joe Piner saying I'd been very quick, and asking me if I was sure I had cut the grass properly.

'Yes', was my reply, 'and now I have to go'.

'What do you mean you have to go?'

'I've been called up, news has just come over the radio'.

I got my cycle and Mrs Hollis came out and gave me my wages, insurance card and an extra £1, and I was gone like a shot. I got home in record time, collected my kit and was away as fast as I could pedal. I was afraid the war was going to finish before I got there. I remember my mother standing on the doorstep, waving goodbye and crying at the same time. Being a young lad that was something I could not understand. It was some time after I found out why. She had seen the horrors of WW1, and wondered if she would ever see me again; after all, she had three sons in the war, Tom, George and now me, the baby of the family. There were also four sons-in-law Joe Griffen married to Rose, Arthur Gatecome, married to Nellie, Bill Troughton to Margaret, and Jack Christy married to Dolly. Brother Jack (his real name was Michael Henry, but he was always known as Jack) was sent back home to carry on with his work of national importance working as a radio engineer at Portishead wireless station near Bristol, and as a radio ham (amateur).

THE WAR YEARS

In 1934 we moved to Highworth in Wiltshire, and it was from there in February 1939 that I joined the Territorial Army. I was a gardener at the time and used to cycle to the drill hall twice a week in Swindon.

On the 3rd of September I reported as requested at the outbreak of war to the drill hall.

The regiment now moved from Tisbury to Baldock in Bedfordshire. At the end of 1939 we received our first 25 pounder guns; eventually we would have twenty four in total. We now started training in earnest. In early 1940, we moved again to Glastonbury in Somerset, and it was when the British Expeditionary Force was withdrawn from Dunkirk in France in June. Over three hundred thousand fighting men were rescued by the little ships which had come together from all over England. These ships were crewed by their owners and by volunteers, and helped to get the men off the beaches to the bigger naval destroyers waiting off shore to take them back to England. It was a truly amazing feat of courage by everyone who volunteered to rescue our beleaguered army.

[*Sgt Albert Figg*]

At the end of June we moved again to Salisbury Plain, it was such wild open countryside, which was wonderful in its own strange way. I loved it when I used to travel through the area on my way to the South West. It is the army tank and infantry training site, and I went there many times with my regiment during the war. I also went to the Royal Artillery Training Centre at Larkhill when I was made a sergeant in 1941. We had to dig slit trenches (and if you have ever had to do that, you will know how very deep with chalk and hard the ground is to dig); it was something I could not understand until it was explained to me that German paratroops may land as part of the German invasion, Operation Sealion, which fortunately did not happen.

From there, in August 1941, we moved to Broadstairs in South East Kent as shore coast gunners to protect the area from possible invasion by Germany. In early September we were repositioned to Sturry near Canterbury as it was found that we were too close to the English Channel to fire field guns. We needed to be at least three and half miles from the coast to be effective. We had to dig gun pits at Westbere, just outside Sturry. We stayed there for two weeks; however, we had very little ammunition, and if the Germans had come we could not have stopped them. It was the British, Polish and other allied Air Forces that saved the day.

In 1941, when the invasion did not happen, we moved to the South East near Margate and carried on training, followed by more training… It was all we seemed to be doing. It was at this time when I was travelling through Kent that, to my surprise, I was seeing young women working in the fields. I was born in Wiltshire in 1920, and it had only ever been men who were farm hands. It was in July/August and they were picking strawberries. I had never seen strawberries growing in fields before; I only thought they were grown in the garden. Later on I saw potatoes being picked; again I had thought they only grew in the garden with the likes of runner beans etc.

Wiltshire was a rich farming county with herds of cows, flocks of sheep, haymaking and many other crops besides, all tended by men; there were never any women in the fields. Women worked as servants in the big houses like my mum did, even when she was married. She no doubt died through working so hard.

[*Group photo of the F subsection; Sgt. Keogh, Bdr. Figg, Lofty Brown, Stan Nelson, Gunner George Webb, and an unknown gentleman.*]

In 1941 I was promoted to a full bombardier [two stripes] and just before Christmas that year we moved again to Wood Street House, near Bapchild/Sittingbourne in Kent. It was there that I met my future wife, Anne Waters, and by October 22, 1942 we were married. It was from there we moved back to the coast at Sandwich into the Bell Hotel. Whilst at Sandwich I got my third stripe, making me the youngest lance sergeant in the regiment. Within three months I was promoted to full sergeant, which meant I could now sew a gun insignia over my three stripes. I had achieved my ambition and beaten my brother George, who had told me that it would take seven years to become a sergeant, and I made it in just three. It shows what one can do if he/she accept a challenge and that has been me all of my life. There is nothing you can't do if you put your mind to it, it's mind over matter. So children, young ladies and gentlemen, learn all you can and take notice of what you teacher tells you, they usually know best. So ends my first lesson.

THE WAR YEARS 57

[*Albert & Anne wedding October 1942*]

[*Group photo of 112 Field Regiment, Royal Artillery, just prior to D-day. (Albert Figg third from the right of the third row).*]

As the war progressed, training intensified. Every man knew exactly what his role was within the gun crew, but he also knew what every other member of the team did. This meant that no matter what happened, if anyone was injured or killed in action we would still be able to carry on manning the guns. As the invasion of Europe got ever closer, we were moved in stages to our final holding points before embarking for France. All leave was cancelled, and we were now locked down, not allowed out of our camp. My excitement grew, but there were nerves as well. Each man reacted in his own way to what was about to happen.

The 112th Field Regiment, The Royal Artillery, wasn't part of the initial landings on the Normandy coast. Other poor sods bore the brunt of the fighting and by the time we landed things were much more organized and calm, though still quite chaotic. We set sail after a three day delay for loading because the dockers went on strike; they wanted danger money for loading live ammo, and there we were going over to Normandy and possibly getting killed. Many were killed, and it made me very angry. I think it was this which gave me the desire to make sure that all of my comrades who did not return are always remembered. We landed on Gold Beach on the 24th June 1944, after being held up in the channel four to five days; we went into action that evening in supporting the 15TH Scottish Division for the first attack on Hill 112. Operation Epsom followed by my Division, 43 Wessex.

On reflection it was rather bizarre; I shall explain. When the landing craft came alongside our ship, the guns and vehicles had been loaded on to the landing craft first and we had to follow by climbing down rope ladders. We got on the landing craft and found it was an American vessel. I was always a bit nervous of the Americans as they were known for not landing you right on the beach and I was particularly worried about that as I could not swim. As number one in the gun team I had to lead my gun on to the beach on foot; that way I would show the driver how deep the water was. I was also rather disconcertingly their mine detector, as I would explode it before my vehicle reached it. My life was expendable, as were the rest of the gun team, the gun, limber and tractor unit plus all the equipment was far more important.

What happened next on the landing craft is something that could only happen with the Americans. Up rolls a marine and asks 'what sort of ice cream would you like, sergeant?' Rather taken aback, I said 'oh, vanilla' without thinking.. and lo and behold an ice cream appeared. Not a word was spoken as we got stuck into the ice cream, and took absolutely no notice of the landing craft moving off. It wasn't until I heard the noise of the ramp crashing down I suddenly realized we were on or very close to the beach. The next thing I was throwing my ice cream away and screaming at my driver to start moving as I ran down the ramp. 'Hang on a minute', I thought to myself, 'Albert, you can't swim!' I stopped to contemplate my next action, but not for long as the quad with the limber and gun was bearing down on me. I had to get out of its way before it ran over me. I just had time to hold my nose and jump. To my great embarrassment, I jumped into about an inch of water. What a fool I felt. I started to run to my left, away from the oncoming vehicle, one of my gunners leant out of the cab and in one swift movement he grabbed and pulled me in to the quad. Not surprisingly it was always a source of great amusement to my gunners that it was the first and last time they manhandled their sergeant.

They were a good bunch of lads and they did their job well. Seven of us came through the war without injuries. Unfortunately, my second driver was killed by friendly fire two days before he was going home on leave in February 1945. It was such a shame. His wife had given birth to twins in September 1944, and he was so much looking forward to seeing them. I made a point of tracking the twins down, and finally met them in 1998. They were so grateful I could give them a firsthand account of how he got killed, but of course not the name of the person who accidentally fired the fatal shot; that will always remain secret. Unfortunately that is what happens in war.

Once ashore we headed south away from the landing beaches. Wherever we went, we would prepare our area for firing the guns. I still have the brass cartridge case from the very first shell I fired against the enemy on the 25th of June, just one day after I landed in France. I also still have my original shaving brush which I still use, though it is a little worse for wear.

On the 6th July I was ordered to go forward with eight men and dig gun pits for our next position, it was known that doing this meant it was going to be a long stay, and possibly under enemy fire. It was a very hot day; the position was in a field just below Carpiquet airfield. We could see the tops of the hangers; the Canadians had only just cleared it of the enemy, and were fighting in the village, we were warned that the enemy could have left snipers there and we may come under fire.

[Albert sitting on a 25-pounder gun in Arromanches. These were similar to the guns he used in the 112 Regiment during te war.]

As it was so hot I let the lads take their shirts off and we started digging. But it wasn't long before I found one of them was missing. Nobody could explain what had happened to him, or maybe they didn't want to split on him. There was nowhere to go except to the airfield; of course, if he got captured or shot I would be on a charge for allowing it to happen. It was no good going to look for him; the job had to be done that day or night and be ready for the battery to move in to them next day. It then started to rain but it was still very hot. There was brilliant sunshine at the same time, but the rain was very welcome. The consequence was sunburn, which we ignored at the time but the skin when it started peeling was very painful for two or three days. We could have been put on a charge for self-inflicted injuries; however, it was all forgotten as it was felt we had suffered enough.

After a while the missing gunner appeared carrying a load of cable and two heavy boxes. I put him on a charge for leaving his post without permission; his answer to this was 'Sarge, I'm going to make digging easy'. He then proceeded to dig a few holes within the perimeter of the pit. I then had the shock of my life; from the boxes he took out sticks of dynamite and detonators. He laid out the cables, inserted the explosive in the holes, connected the cable and placed the detonators. Oh my God… He lit the fuse and we all ran like hell! There were five very loud bangs and the clods of soil went everywhere and rained down on us. I thought Jerry would hear it and then start shelling, but no, thankfully nothing happened. As a result of the ingenuity of that gunner, we had all the pits prepared in record time.

When you are digging gun pits you only go down approximately twelve inches and the soil put all around the outside makes it another twelve inches higher, to stop shrapnel. I never did press the charges against the gunner and nobody was any the wiser. There are times when in charge of men you have to give and take a little, but he got a bloody good telling off nonetheless.

On the night 6/7th July we moved into the prepared gun pits. It was a nice and sunny warm morning. Unfortunately there were no buildings where we could sleep or brew up, so we had sit around the gun and lay down under the sky. It was sometime later, on that afternoon of the 7th, that we heard and saw a very large number of aircraft approaching. The sky was black. They must have been at less than a thousand feet; it seemed that they were directly overhead when they opened their bomb bay doors and the bombs came raining down. To us it seemed as if they were coming straight for us. We all dived for cover in the gun pit with our hands over our heads thinking it was the end for us. I had never seen bombs dropping before, so didn't know that they followed the path of the planes. After a while, when we heard a crunching noise we looked up and saw the bombs going towards Caen. The sky was like night time, black with smoke and flames, all you could see was the outline of the planes and the noise of explosions. The people of Caen must have gone through hell. I was given to understand that over 6000 civilians including children were killed, but very few Germans. They had pulled back before the bombing started; they knew what was coming, and when the bombing stopped they moved back in. When the Canadians started to advance to capture Caen the tanks could not help because of debris caused by the bombing. All the streets were impassable by vehicles so it was hand-to-hand fighting, and the Canadians had heavy losses. It was considered that the bombing should not have happened and was an unnecessary waste of life.

It was after the bombing I decided I needed to go to the latrine. You have no doubt heard of being so scared you nearly shit yourself… well that was me. I arrived at the latrines, a trench dug in the ground with a pole set above it, and had to find a clean spot to sit down. I sat down and started to read the paper, when all of a sudden a loud noise of a shell came over the top. It dropped about 200m behind me will terrific explosion, then a few seconds later another came over, this time was too close for comfort. I didn't wait for the next one. I shot off the pole like a scolded cat and ran up to my gun still with the paper in my hand and my trousers around my ankles. My gunners were shouting, at the top of their voices, 'turn around sarge and fire from your rear end! If our shells don't kill Jerry perhaps you may be able to gas them!'

It was on the 9th July we started receiving very large quantities of ammunition. Usually it was brought to us by our own transport, but this time the Army Service Corps brought ammunition to us, lorry upon lorry. By the time they had delivered it all, it was stacked head high. It was the start of Operation Jupiter; we started firing at 0430 on the morning of the 10th July. (The story can be found on on www.hill112.com)

THE BATTLE FOR HILL 112.

Introduction

I was a sergeant in the Royal Field Regiment of Artillery with a twenty-five pounder Howitzer gun. Our role as gunners was to support the infantry and tanks on the battlefield. When they were advancing into enemy territory, we would fire a barrage initially to soften up the enemy. Then we would fire a creeping barrage, firing just ahead of the advancing soldiers and armour to protect them and to force the enemy to withdraw. This process would continue until our infantry had captured their objective.

Our range was approximately six miles, but in most cases we would be three and a half miles behind the infantry (we were known by the infantry as 'the Five Mile Snipers'). We would never see our own shells fall, so I have never known how many of the enemy were killed as a result of our work, and nor do I want to.

I think that most of you will have heard of Operation Overlord, which was the code name given to the invasion and liberation of Western Europe from Nazi Germany. The liberation started on the 6th of June 1944, better known as D-Day. The code name Overlord referred to the whole operation, but within it there were offensives that were also given code names to differentiate them, such as Epsom, Jupiter and Goodwood, to name just a few.

The battles I will concentrate on are Epsom and Jupiter. But, before I go any further, I would like to start from the beginning. When Operation Overlord started there were three British beaches named Gold, Juno and Sword. To the west, on our right, were the Americans on Omaha and Utah. For simplicity, I will mention only the division, primary the 50th Northumbrian, who landed on Gold beach on the morning of the sixth. Their task was to secure the beach then fight inland and sideways to join up with the other beaches. Other divisions were doing the same on the other beaches, and as a result they would create a solid front line of some fifty miles and then start advancing to form a beachhead. This would allow further troops, tanks, & guns, and most important the infantry (known as footsloggers) It can now be said that the invasion had been successful after two weeks of fierce fighting, with heavy loss of lives on both sides, however, I have been given to understand from historians, and from the many books I have read since, that in this war there were many more Germans lost than the Allies,

Early days in Normandy: An overview account of Albert's division in the context of the battle

The capture of the principal city in Lower Normandy, Caen, had been a D-Day objective for the 3rd (British) Division landing across 'Sword' Beach between the port of Ouistreham and the seaside resort of Lion-sur-Mer. The intervention of the German 21st Panzer Division had prevented this, and the task became further beyond reach with the arrival of the 12th (SS) Panzer Division the following day, 7th June, and for the next month the 3rd Division's attempts at a frontal assault were blocked by the same opponents.

Further to the west, despite a very bloody assault landing by the US 1st and 29th Divisions on 6th June, the 26th Infantry from the 1st Division had advanced as far south as Caumont, almost 20 miles from the coast, capturing the town on 13th June. On the same day in the British Sector, the 7th Armoured Division, the renowned 'Desert Rats', were launched to exploit this perceived gap, and form the western half of the pincer to encircle Caen. The eastern half was found by the 51st Highland Division, another of General Montgomery's favourite divisions brought back with him from the Mediterranean theatre. The attack by two battalions of 152 Brigade was virtually still-born, stopped by stubborn defence and an unusually strong and heavy artillery bombardment.

Nevertheless, over the next six days, with newly arrived divisions, sufficient progress was made to enable General Montgomery to feel confident that a secure lodgement had been achieved in Normandy, and that he had drawn in the main German reserves. In England, on the 14th June, Albert Figg's Regiment, 112 Field Regiment, left Eastbourne unannounced to the local population, among whom the soldiers had lived since

January of that year. Early on a fine sunny morning, convoys of the regiment's vehicles drove north through Kent en route for the marshalling area of Tilbury, and an unexplained wait that is a bane of the troops lives. The loading onto the transport ship complete, the regiment sailed for Normandy, arriving off the coast on the 20th.

The weather was now to intervene with the worst storm in forty years blowing in the English Channel, disrupting the smooth flow of logistic supplies, the landing of more troops, and entirely destroying the artificial harbour constructed by American forces, 'Mulberry A'. Among those troops was 112 Field Regiment, to endure three miserable days in heavy seas and many cases of severe seasickness. Meanwhile, General Montgomery had planned another pincer attack on Caen, with the main weight in the western or right-hand half undertaken by the newly arriving VIII Corps, of which Albert's regiment was a small cog, with the operation planned to begin on 22nd June, a date on which the weather was not consulted. Instead, Operation 'Epsom', as it was known, would open on 26th June, by which time the following forces would comprise VIII Corps:

11th Armoured Division
15th (Scottish) and 43rd (Wessex) Infantry Divisions
4th Armoured Brigade and 31 Tank Brigade
8th AGRA (Army Group Royal Artillery)

A force of some 60,000 troops.

Within this strong force, the relevant component was 43rd (Wessex) Division, as its name implies, consisting of County regiments and units with their roots in the West Country. The division itself was made up three brigades, each consisting of three infantry battalions, an artillery field regiment and engineer and medical units. Then there was a large logistical element, 'slices' of which supported the fighting 'teeth' of the division, its three brigades. The three brigades were numbered, 129, 130 and 214, of which 130 Brigade is the one that concerns the reader. 4th and 5th Battalions, The Dorset Regiment and 7th Battalion (The Hampshire) made up that brigade, for which the artillery unit was 112 Field Regiment. Similarly each battery of 112 Field provided close support to one infantry battalion, 477 Battery to 4th Dorsets, and 217 Battery, 7th Hampshires,. 220 Battery to 5th Dorsets, and Albert's battery, 477 to 4th Dorsets.

Operation 'EPSOM'

VIII Corps was commanded by General O'Connor who had been captured during the fighting in North Africa, but who had subsequently escaped. His plan called for 15th (Scottish) Division to break out through ground already captured and held by 3rd (Canadian) Infantry Division and to secure crossings over the river Odon between the villages of Gavrus and Verson, with the intermediate objective of the capture of the villages of St Manvieux and Cheux. In the event of opposition being light in the early stages, then 11th Armoured Division would be unleashed to rush to seize the crossings over the River Odon. But should the armour not succeed in rushing the crossings, 15th (Scottish) Division's second objective would be to advance and hold these river crossings. Should the crossings not be intact, then it became the division's responsibility to construct crossings strong enough to carry armoured traffic and a fifth bridge for lighter vehicles and infantry on foot.

For all these tasks additional troops were placed under command of 15th (Scottish) Division:

> *Two regiments of Churchill infantry tanks of 31st Tank Brigade*
> *Two squadrons of flail (mine-clearing) tanks, a squadron from each of 22 dragoons and Westminster Dragoons*
> *A squadron of specialised armoured engineers of 81st Squadron*
> *A battery of self-propelled 17-pdr tank destroyers from 91st Anti-Tank Regiment.*

The task of 11th Armoured Division was to attempt to rush the River Odon crossings and establish themselves on the high ground to the south of the river, and subsequently, in phase two of the operation, to force a passage over the River Orne, thus blocking the escape route of the German defenders in Caen. For these tasks, the division was to be supported by the three armoured regiments and one motorised infantry battalion of 4th Armoured Brigade, plus another battery from 91st Anti-Tank Regiment.

43rd (Wessex) Division would meanwhile come into play, and provide the 'firm base' for the Corps, by filling in to take over the ground captured by 15th (Scottish Division).

A most impressive element with the corps was the largest concentration of guns so far employed on the whole of the Allied, British and US, front. The concentration was found by:

11th Armoured Division	Two field regiments, 48 guns
15th (Scottish) Division	Four field regiments (including the additional 25th Field Regiment, 96 guns
43rd (Wessex) Division	Three field regiments (94th, 112th and 179th), 72 guns
4th Armoured Brigade	One fieldr, 24 guns
8th AGRA	One heavy regiment, 16 guns
	One medium, 16 guns
	One heavy anti-aircraft regiment, 24 guns

Also available, if in range were 216th Field, 32nd Medium and 16 heavy guns of 1st Corps, and from XXX Corps, 96 field, 64 medium and 16 heavy guns. What is more, the Royal Navy could provide the monitor HMS Roberts and three cruisers.

Weather permitting, a force of heavy bombers and another of medium bombers, would undertake attacks to safeguard the left flank of the attack area, and fifteen squadrons of fighter bombers would maintain strong fighter cover. In the event, adverse weather did not allow the bombing element, although fighters were available as soon as the weather broke.

The morning of 26th June dawned dull and hazy, and preceded by an intense artillery barrage 46th (Highland) Infantry Brigade with 7th Royal Tanks advanced on the village of Cheux and Haut du Bosq , and 44th (Lowland) Brigade with 9th Royal Tanks on St Manvieu and La Gaule.

Very happy to move from the first gun positions near a shattered dairy, and the foul smell of a lake on rancid milk and bloated dead cattle, the guns moved forward during the night of 25th June, and at 8.00 am on the morning of the 26th, the opening day of the battle 112 Field Regiment and Albert's Section (gun) fired their first rounds as the Scottish infantry moved across their start line, going forward into the attack. Despite hostile fire from well-concealed positions, soon after mid-day, the infantry of 2nd Glasgow Highlanders were clearing houses and orchards in the straggling village of Cheux while, on their right, 9th Cameronians cleared the enemy as they advanced on Haut du Bosq. On their left, the Lowlanders of 8th Royal Scots and 6th Royal Scots Fusiliers tackled St Manvieu and the hamlet of La Gaule on the Caen – Fontenay road.

By midday on the 26th it seemed that all was going to plan. However, it later transpired that the four villages had been held as an outpost line and to emphasise how thinly spread was the enemy, 12th (SS) Panzer Division, the outposts had been held by the Division's Engineer Battalion. These were elite troops whose specialist expertise was wasted in the way the Battalion was employed. It was also about this time the enemy brought heavy mortar fire down, taking a heavy toll on the attacking troops

Despite its gun positions being well behind the infantry's start line, Albert's regiment was not immune from random shelling as German artillery ranged on the abundant targets.

During the afternoon of the first day of the operation, units of 15th (Scottish) Division were finding progress difficult, south of the captured villages. At 18.00 orders were therefore given for the division's third brigade, 227th (Highland) to advance, 10th HLI on the right towards Grainville and 1st Gordons, left, on Colleville, each battalion to be supported by the leading regiments of 29th Armoured Brigade of 11th (Armoured) Division, 2nd Fife and Forfar Yeomanry and 23rd Hussars respectively. Once the two villages were secured, then 2nd Argylls would move forward to take Le Valtru. Heavy rain fell as daylight faded on what had been very limited further progress.

The plan for the 27th June remained the development of the previous evening's plan, and once the crossings over the river Odon had been secured for 11th (Armoured) Division they were able to pass through and dominate the high ground beyond before the final bound towards the River Orne.

Overnight, 112th Field moved forward in filthy weather doing its best to avoid setting up its new positions on top of a minefield, which had been laid to protect the Canadian positions that had formed the start for 15th (Scottish) Division advance 24 hours earlier. The battle raging all day further south was supported by the artillery of the divisions involved, thus it was not until the morning of the 29th that the guns of 112th Field would again fire in anger.

Not so their fellow gunners of 179 Field Regiment in 43 (Wessex) Division, supporting the 5th Duke of Cornwall's Light Infantry. On the morning of the 27th, the Duke of Cornwall's had moved forward to begin the process of forming the 'firm base' by taking over positions from the Scots infantry, by occupying the fields and orchards around Haut du Bosq. But as soon as they began their advance they were engaged from the right and the direction of Rauray. The neighbouring division on the right, 49th Infantry Division, the 'Polar Bears' after their characteristic formation arm badge (and reflecting earlier service in Iceland) had not succeeded in advancing far enough south to give the protection planned. Worse, arriving to take over their positions, it was found that the 9th Cameronians had already vacated their positions, so the Duke of Cornwall's found themselves having to deal with tenacious individuals from the highly indoctrinated Hitler Youth of 12th (SS) Panzer Division, still lurking in the area. Yet worse was to come when heavily armed and powerful Panther tanks rumbled into the orchard occupied by the Dukes' headquarters. It was the infantry that recovered from their surprise first and after brisk engagements; five of the six tanks had been destroyed or disabled and the one survivor had turned tail. In their first engagement, 5th Duke of Cornwall's were the talk of VIII Corps.

Elsewhere, to the south of this remarkable battle, 10th Highland Light Infantry and the tanks of 2nd Fife and Forfar were finding tough opposition delaying their southward progress, although by midday a squadron of the Fife and Forfar did managed to get into the village of Grainville and hold it for several hours.

Better progress was made on the left flank by 2nd Gordons and 23rd Hussars' tanks, and against less resistance, by 10.00 am 2nd Argyll and Sutherland Highlanders had moved through Colleville to reach the main east-west road out of Caen, at this stage being used unconcernedly by German transports units between Caen and towns to the west. Pressing on, but making slow progress clearing pockets of enemy from countryside ideal for defence, by 17.00 leading troops of 2nd Argylls had reached the banks of the River Odon. Covered by tanks of 23rd Hussars, a small bridgehead was now established.

Further north, the infantry of 43rd (Wessex) Division moved forward to positions to strengthen the firm base that 5th Duke of Cornwall's had begun to create. During the late evening more infantry were on the move south, this time the three battalions of 159 Infantry Brigade, the other major component of 11th (Armoured) Division. (At this stage of the campaign, while infantry divisions were comprised of 3 brigades, an armoured dvision was comprise of two, one infantry, the other armoured.)

By nightfall, on the second day, 27th June, VIII Corps troops had secured crossings over the River Odon, and were poised to execute the next phase of the operation, the seizing of the high ground above the villages of Evrecy and Esquay, preliminary to the next and final phase, crossings over the much larger River Orne.

After a challenging advance at night through ground as yet unseen, and without knowing what or where the enemy lay in wait, as the gloom of dawn of 28th June dispersed 1st Herefordshire Regiment and 4th King's Shropshire Light Infantry has crossed the River Odon and were organising a wider bridgehead south of the bridge at Tourmanville and on the lower slopes of the ground rising to what were labelled as Hills 112 and 113, but were more like a plateaux. 3rd Monmouthshire Regiment reinforced the northern bank of the Odon.

As soon as the light made it possible two squadrons of 23rd Hussars were ordered to advance up the slopes and establish themselves on the top of Hill 112, having disposed, with the held of the accompanying Company of 8th Rifle Brigade, of enemy on the crest of the hill. Even with the arrival of 23rd Hussars third squadron later in the morning, the regiment could not make any further progress because of the Germans occupying the southern, and reverse, slopes of Hill 112, and a small wood where Tiger tanks were dug in and able to move under cover to alternative positions. At around 1500hr, 3rd Royal Tanks came forward to relieve 23rd Hussars who by now were beginning to run short of ammunition, and it was otherwise not possible for soft-skinned lorries to replenish stocks.

While the end of the day marked no further progress towards the next river line if the Orne, many minor battles had been fought north of the River Odon, and ominous signs that a vigorous German reaction was in its early stages, with prisoner identification and interrogation revealing the arrival of the 2nd (SS) Das Reich Division, harried all the way in their journey from the south of France. South of the river the bridgehead had been enlarged and a second crossing at Gavrus secured by 2nd Argylls.

Nevertheless, although General O'Connor had in mind maintaining the intention of the operation, lack of progress on both flanks by 49th Division in the west and 3rd (Canadian) nearer Caen had caused VIII to have created a significant salient. Thus, on the 29th June, the corps passed to the defensive, with intelligence indicating the imminence of that vigorous reaction.

In contrast, two of the three brigades of 43rd (Wessex) Division made aggressive moves by 129th Brigade consolidating positions south of St Manvieux and 1st Worcesters of 214th Brigade executing what was considered to be a textbook attack to capture the village of Mouen. While these moves were supported by 94th and 179th Field Regiments, 112th Field contributed a barrage of 86 rounds per gun – over 2,000 shells landing over perhaps 40 minutes. In fact the attack by

1st Worcesters also had the effect of disrupting an attack by a second SS Panzer Division, 1st, to be sucked into containing the VIII Corps salient.

Enemy activity in the west increased pressure on two of 15th (Scottish) Division Brigades north of the River Odon, while forward of the river 29th Armoured Brigade had a difficult day. In their attempt to extend the hold on the westerly Hill 113 plateau, 44 royal tanks from 4th Armoured Brigade had a torrid time losing thirteen tanks and three more damaged – the equivalent to one third of its tank strength in a single afternoon. The original plan had envisaged both 29th Armoured and 4th Armoured Brigades being between the Rivers Odon and Orne, but in view of the increased pressure being exerted from the south-west, 4th Armoured Brigade, less the unfortunate 44 royal tanks, were deployed to support 46th (Highland) Brigade. That the enemy had reinforced this sector was confirmed by prisoner identification revealing the presence of another Regiment of 1 SS Panzer Division.

While the day had been marked by the increase in artillery fire in both directions, the majority was towards the Germans. The very considerable threat from 2nd SS Panzer Corps, consisting of yet two more SS Panzer Divisions, 9th (Hohenstaufen) and 10th (Frundsberg), whose presence was known through the top secret 'Ultra' signal intelligence, had brought their artillery guns. Repeated calls for defensive fire were made on the corps artillery, who responded magnificently. Yet the 72 guns of 43rd (Wessex) were not part of this. With the reality of the threat from 2nd SS Panzer Corps in mind, orders came in the evening to 112 Field to vacate their gun pits and take up positions in an anti-tank role facing towards the south-west.

To their front 44th (Lowland) Brigade was taking the brunt of the attack north of the River Odon by 9th (SS) Panzer, making better progress than 10th (SS) south of the river. It had been the intention that these attacks be made much earlier in the day, and while the start was made in the early afternoon even that attempt could not get going. The reason for the disruption was the persistent attacks by fighter bombers.

Nevertheless, in anticipation of further concerted enemy attacks the following day, General O'Connor ordered the withdrawal of 29th Armoured Brigade from its exposed positions south of the River Odon, a decision endorsed by General Dempsey, the army commander. It was a blow to 11th (Armoured) Division, who had not been defeated, to give up ground so hardly won. Between 23.00hr on the 29th and 04.00hr on the 30th, in pouring rain, the withdrawal of four armoured regiments across a single bridge with steep, narrow approaches was accomplished with great skill and professionalism. What was more, the move went without interference from the enemy.

If the 29th June marked the end of VIII Corps offensive intentions before achieving the original aim of the partial encirclement of Caen from the south and west, Operation Epsom had the achieved the effect of sucking in one enemy armoured formation after another and preventing their use en masse.

From VIII Corps perspective, it formed a formidable defence in depth, and the 30th June saw the continuation of German efforts to break this down. If the strong enemy attacks the previous day, 29th June had caused over 600 casualties across the Corps, the ferocity of German efforts on the 30th June can be illustrated by the casualty figure rising to close on 1,100.

Sadly, some 250 of these occurred to units of 43rd (Wessex) Division. By 30th June, 129 Brigade had come forward, 5th Wiltshires were occupying the straggling village of Baron and 4th Somersets the wooded area on the road east to Fontaine Étoupefour. 4th Wiltshires were in reserve in the woods to the east of Tourville. But for the efforts of the sweating gunners of all three of the divisions artillery regiments the numbers could have been higher, had not their shellfire broken up the enemy's infantry attacks. If 129th Brigade suffered from the vicious mortar fire from the German's multi-barrelled 'Nebelwerfers', the numbers of casualties inflicted on the German assailants can be imagined. Albert's neighbouring 220th battery records firing over 1,000 rounds of high explosive (HE) on the 29th and 30th June.

The Odon Bridgehead

As July opened, 43rd (Wessex) Division had two brigades astride or south of the line of the river Odon, while 130th Brigade remained in reserve around the stinking village of Cheux. The guns of 112th Field had returned to their earlier positions near Le Mesnil Patry.

For the next four days, the forward brigades fended off probing attacks and the guns of all three regiments were constantly in action bringing down fire to break up any attempts by the enemy to attack in any strength. 'Uncle' targets, when all 72 guns of the division were in action were common, Albert's gun detachment firing on average 200 rounds each day.

On 5th July came the Regiment's next move, its fourth, to follow reconnaissance and digging parties to prepare new gun positions forward of St Manvieu, captured by Royal Scots and Royal Scots Fusiliers on 26th June, the opening day of 'Epsom'.

220th Battery had the misfortune to occupy gun positions that were very exposed and under observation from enemy occupying positions on Carpiquet airfield. Some respite was had when Canadian troops cleared the enemy out the following day.

At the same time, the infantry of 130th Brigade moved forward to take over positions, which they were to occupy until 9th July, south of the River Odon from 159th Infantry Brigade. These positions had been under constant threat from enemy attacks, all of which had been broken up by 'Victor' and 'Yoke' targets, the latter being when every gun within range was brought to bear.

Meanwhile the gun lines of 112th Field had not been immune from retaliatory artillery fire, and on the 2nd July, Gnr Atkins was the first casualty in 477th Battery when hit in the legs by shrapnel.

Senior commanders within 43dr (Wessex) Division had been given advanced warning that the division was to undertake its first major attack, as a division as a whole, on 10th July, and the days in between were used for planning, going forward to try to see the ground where the attacks would take place, and to prepare orders so that all the troops new what jobs they had to do. For the gun numbers there was hard work humping ammunition as it was brought forward in trucks and stockpiled in preparation for the big attack to come.

On 7th July, troops of the division had almost grandstand seats to observe the first use of massed bombers to support the ground forces attacks, when in the evening over 400 aircraft appeared in the north-east to bomb targets to the north of the city of Caen. It was a huge boost to morale for Albert and his gun crew to see this demonstration of power and destruction. Sadly, far more destruction than intended fell on the city itself causing hundreds of innocent civilian deaths. Flames of burning buildings could be seen lasting through the night of the 7/8th July.

In preparation for 'Operation Jupiter', as it was known, the infantry battalions of 130th Brigade had handed over their positions to the Scots and moved back. Late on the 9th, transport brought the attacking troops back to debus before lying in the dark for their last meal to come up. They then made their final move to the start line for the attack, for which 'Zero Hour' was 0500hr on the morning of the 10th July.

Operation 'JUPITER'

VIII Corps intention was laid down as:

"At 0500 hours, Monday 10th July, 8th Corps will attack and seize the area Baron – Hill 112 – junction with the River Orne (east of Maltot) with a view to a subsequent exploitation south-west of the high ground east of the River Ajon" (sic)

The main attacking role was this time given to 43rd (Wessex) Division, the Division's task being:

"43rd Division with under command:
    4th Armoured Brigade
    31st Tank Brigade
    46th (Highland) Brigade (from 15th Division)
is to carry out the attack in four phases:

Phase 1.	Capture of the area Fontaine Etoupefour - Chateau de Fontaine - Hill 112 - Baron
Phase 2.	Capture and clear Eterville
Phase 3.	Capture of the area of Maltot to the River Orne
Phase 4.	On completion of Phase 3 an armoured Regimental Group is to pass to the south through the infantry and report the presence or otherwise of the enemy in the area of the half dozen or so villages to the west of the River Orne. Infantry is then to follow up 4th Armoured Brigade quickly in order to consolidate the final line as soon as possible.

Timings:

0500 hrs	H Hour
0600 hrs	Phase 1 complete
0615 hrs	Phase 2
0715 hrs	Phase 2 complete
0800 hrs	Phase 3
0900 hrs	Phase 3 complete
	4 Armoured Brigade to be prepared to operate in Phase 4 from 0900 hrs.

Artillery and Air Support
8 AGRA, plus, under command 3 AGRA.

RAF task to interdict on enemy movement on roads leading to the area of operations, and provide continuous on call support on selected targets, such as Maltot, Evrecy, Esquay, Bully etc."

10th July 1944 would be a memorable day for all those who were there.

For Sgt Albert Figg's gun detachment, in 477th Battery, 112th Field Regiment, the day's work started at ten minutes before Zero Hour with a massive artillery barrage delivered by some 700 guns. The opening fire order of the day was for fifty rounds fired at the rate of five rounds per minute, twenty-five pounds of high explosive bursting every twelve seconds from that one gun barrel alone.

At the same time as two Dorset Battalions went into action, the three battalions of 129 Brigade, 4th and 5th Wiltshires and 4th Somersets set off from the straggling village of Baron, occupied by 7th Hampshires on 4th July, to follow the line of a track that was an old Pilgrim's Way up the slopes of Hill 112 towards a small Calvary at the top. Despite their best efforts all day, the Phase 1 objective of the capture of Hill 112 remained beyond their grasp.

As 5th Dorsets advanced from their positions behind the village of Fontaine Étoupefour to attack a group of buildings at Les Dauns, the eight guns of 477th Battery brought fire down ahead of the advancing infantry, altering their gun sights every three minutes so that their fire matched the rate of the infantry's progress. There was a brief respite on the gun as the infantry fought for possession of the buildings of the Chateau de Fontaine against stubborn resistance by a Company of 12th (SS) Panzer Division. Then, an hour later at 0800, two companies of 5th Dorsets started to move forward on the left of 7th Hampshires on the village of Maltot, and in concert with 277th Battery, the two batteries repeated the creeping barrage of five rounds per minute for the next hour.

It was clear from the number and frequency of calls from forward observers for artillery fire to be brought down that the Hampshire and Dorset infantrymen were experiencing a very difficult time, and that capture of the village of Maltot was not going to be as easy as the attacks on Chateau de Fontaine, and on the village of Eterville by 4th Dorsets. And for five solid hours gun numbers sweated with the hard physical labour of serving their guns to help the hard-pressed infantry to keep their tenuous hold on the village.

By early evening it became clear that 4th Dorsets going forward into Maltot had merely reinforced failure, and orders were given for withdrawal. To help the battle-weary troops get away, the entire corps artillery of 240 guns was bringing fire down at the rapid rate on the area just beyond the village.

As the light of a very long day faded, there was still a job for 5th Duke of Cornwall's. The two other battalions, 1st Worcesters and 7th Somersets of 214th Brigade had come up to take over the ground across which 5th Dorsets had attacked earlier in the day. As a 'final throw of the dice' General Thomas, commanding 43rd (Wessex) Division sent his last available unit to take the summit of the Hill. Not for nothing was the small wood surmounting the hill to become known as 'Cornwall Wood', and what had been the little Calvary again convey its original significance.

It was fortunate that the enemy, too had been exhausted by the day and no attempts were made to follow up the troops withdrawing to the area around Château de Fontaine. At last, after some sixteen hours of constant, energy-sapping demands, gun numbers could have time for a cup of tea, later very sad to learn that among the very heavy losses suffered, particularly by the infantry: 4th Dorsets ended the day 70 strong; 7th Hampshires incurred 226 casualties, and that 47th Battery had not been immune. Two of the team of 4th in the battery's OP party were wounded, Gnr Carpendale later dying of his wounds.

At the end of the day, the corps objectives had been by no means achieved. Subsequent days were to see 15th (Scottish) and 53rd (Welsh) Divisions come forward and try to take the advance on to the west of Hill 112. But for 4rd3(Wessex) Division it was time to lick their wounds, recover, and absorb reinforcements, all the while holding forward positions on the line of the road between Caen and Evrecy. And it would be another fortnight before the division was relieved.

10th July 1944 would be a date long remembered by those soldiers of 43rd (Wessex) Infantry Division who fought that day and lived to fight another day.

The wartime Minister of Defence Sir James Griggs report

As the centre of events moved westwards, the advantageous and remarkable views of Hill 112 lost their relevance. On 4th August 1944, after all the blood spilt down its slopes, Hill 112 fell into the hands of the 53rd Welsh Division on the 23rd August with hardly a fight (in fact the Germans vacated the hill).

Let the words of War Minister Sir James Griggs report to the House of Commons have the final say on the six weeks of fighting at Hill 112.

Meanwhile, the British and the Canadians, though making some local gains, were primarily concerned with holding the hinge position south-west of Caen and containing the greater part of the enemies available armour. To them had been assigned the unspectacular task of forming the anvil upon which the German forces were held and pounded to destruction.

As I was part of the 43rd Wessex division, this is how I saw it. The 43rd Wessex Division was the main division that started Operation Jupiter, after Operation Epsom finished on the 30th June 1944. On 10th July, Jupiter started; during that time there was what was known as a stalemate. This is just what Field Marshal Montgomery wanted. He knew that the Americans had to capture the port of Cherbourg to allow their supplies to come from America straight to the port instead of going to England and then back to Normandy. The American's Mulberry Harbour had been destroyed in the gale, ours however, was only damaged and was soon repaired. It was an impossible position: our harbour could not manage by supplying both at the same time, therefore, the stalemate continue until the harbour had been captured.

It was after its capture in Operation Cobra, then started by the Americans, that Montgomery simultaneously ordered the final attack on Hill 112 and also Operation Goodwood, by taking away the 11th Armoured Division, a very big mistake on his part, as the division was almost destroyed. However, the final attack on Hill 112 was making good progress and by the 23rd August it fell into the hands of the 53rd Welsh Division.

After crossing the river Seine, the bridge had been destroyed, we arrived at a place called Vernon in the late afternoon with the Wiltshire Regiment and the Somerset, plus tanks of the Sherwood Foresters and the Engineers.

We had travelled so fast, the enemy did not know we were there, it was about midnight, and it was thought that there would be very little resistance when the Wiltshire's made their first attack. Although mainly armed with heavy machine guns and what was left of their heavy artillery and tanks etc. after the battle at the Falais Gap, they had retreated towards Belgium and Holland.

The Wiltshire's lost a lot of men from drowning in the Seine, so they had to move down stream to find another easier place to cross, which they did, at the same time the Somerset's made their crossing to the left of the destroyed bridge, however, they set off and had no trouble from the enemy and in time all landed, they thought they were in luck with no casualties, but, when morning arrived they found they were on an island in the middle of the Seine, which meant that they had to start again, and this time they managed to land the other side with few casualties, however, the very the little resistance that was made it was thought that the enemy was running away fast.

This proves my theory that Hill 112 was the most important battle fought in Normandy, because, when the Hill was vacated by the Germans after the battle for Mount Pincon and Falais Gap, the evidence of the enemy's losses were there for all to see. The sights along the roads have stayed with me ever since. I remember it was a very hot day as we travelled past the carnage, and the smell as a result of the heat was horrendous; I had to wet my handkerchief and put it over my mouth. Everywhere you looked there were dead horses, cattle, German soldiers, burnt out tanks, smashed artillery guns, trucks and everything else pertaining to the detritus of war. The 43rd Wessex Division travelled approximately 120 miles without firing a shot.

Before I forget, I must tell you a little story which at the time was amusing, but not afterwards. We went into a gun position along the side of a small side rail track, and found our location was right in front of railway hut. This was just the job; it gave some cover if it was cold or raining without us having to sit on the gun when not firing. We never did fire our guns during the whole of the time there, due to the fact we had trees around us and our shells would have exploded on impact with them and caused casualties. There in that little hut, we were making a cup tea by boiling the water on a small primus stove we'd found when a Frenchman came up shouting and waving his arms. None of us could speak French, so we carried on as if nothing was happening. I thought he was angry because we were trespassing in *his* hut… That did it! Here we were liberating them, and he was upset over a bloody hut. With that, I had had enough of his blabbing so I picked up my Sten gun and shot a round into the air. You've never seen someone run so fast, but he was still waving his arms and shouting. It was then that one of my gunners shouted 'Sergeant, I believe he said something about gasoline'. I looked around to see what he was talking about, and couldn't see anything until I looked at a drum the primus stove was sat on, still boiling some water… Oh my god! I picked up the still flaming primus stove and without thinking threw the whole lot out of the hut, including the tea which we'd already made and the cups. Good job they were made of tin; on taking the cap off the drum, we found it was full of petrol. We survived to tell the tale, and the petrol certainly came in handy for our next journey.

All we were told was that we had to fill up with as much fuel as we could, and take spare jerrycans with us as our journey would take two days. We also had to pack our compo rations. (A compo pack contained enough rations to last two days for the six men in the vehicle), and make sure all our water bottles were filled. At this stage I should mention that, when the Seine crossing had been made, the whole of the British Army went through and within three weeks had captured Antwerp, Brussels, and Paris. At that stage we thought we were on the way to victory by the end of the year; as you will see, that did not happen.

We made our way along the road, bypassing these three cities, and shortly after that another funny thing happened. Believe me, all wars are serious; but incidents like the one I'm about to tell you release the tension. We were travelling in what was known as close order, telephone posts used as a measurement. This was that each gun and vehicle should be two posts apart about 60 yards. We had travelled several miles when we were ordered to close to 30 yards; apparently the German Air Force had been able to increase its presence. It was the first time that the Luftwaffe had been around in any sort of force since before D-day. Anyway we were not attacked, but what happened was that as everyone was travelling at 60 yards it was quite a while before we managed close up and in the meantime the RASC (Royal Army Service Corps) were in a hurry, and one of them managed to get between me and the next gun in front. At first I was angry until I saw what was in the back of it. I couldn't believe my luck; I told my driver to drive up as close as he could. 'Why?', came back the question, as he looked at me with surprise. 'Shut up and do as you're told', I said, with my sergeant's voice. It was only when he got as close as he could that he saw what was in the back of the lorry. I can hear now, all these years later, saying 'bloody hell, how are we going get it?'

The lorry was full of compo packs; could we liberate a few? Well, we would give it our best shot. The only way we could get to them was for me to climb out of the hatch in the roof of my quad. Someone always had to stand there, day or night, to keep a close look out and help the driver if things got tight. I managed get on to the bonnet and walk carefully to the front and then get hold of the tail board of the vehicle in front. I grabbed hold of one box, and one of my gunners standing in the hatch reached forward and managed to grab it from me. Unfortunately, I only had time for just the one box before the driver of the truck started to move out to pass the next gun and quad; such a pity. Now believe me or not, it only took a few seconds to get back down inside the quad and the compo pack had disappeared. 'Where the hell is the pack?' I asked. 'We've packed it away in the lockers', came the reply. I am sure they were all magicians, as even the cardboard box had vanished. It also turned out to be comp pack 'A' which contained tinned fruit, chocolate, cigarettes, matches and a lot more besides. It was cheers all round.

OPERATION MARKET GARDEN.

Here I would like to explain that Market was the code name for the airborne, and the land operation by 30 Corps was Garden.

The Garden Operation envisaged that the Guards Armoured Division breaking out of the bridgehead over the Canal linking up with the three A/B .Divisions and the 43rd Wessex Division to take over the advance to capture the area of Apeldoorn to the north over the Rhine and reach the Zuider Zee. Should any of the five bridges be blown, the 43rd would be called up for an assault crossing and bridging of the Rhine. For this operation the five artillery regiments were reinforced by the 147 Essex Yeomanry Field Regiment, 8th Armoured Brigade, 64th Medium Regiment, 9th Heavy Battery, and a gun troop from the Royal Netherland Princess Irene Brigade.

After the crossing of the river Seine by the Wiltshire Regiment, the 43rd went into a rest period and regrouped with new men, after losing so many during the battles in Normandy and beyond. It was around about the 14th of September 1944. We set off and made our way through Belgium, finishing up at a village called Neerpelt just to the east of the borders of Belgium and Holland. We moved into a field known by the locals as 'the factory', due to the tall chimneys. I always made my gunners dig a slit trench, no matter what time we went into action, day or night. We normally were able to go down approximately two feet; however, on this occasion we kept digging and digging but the sides kept falling in. So what could we do to stop it? Just because I was a sergeant it doesn't mean I knew everything… In fact, far from it. Most of my gunners were older than me, and knew more about digging on soft ground than I did. One gunner suggested we 'revet' the slit trench. I know we all looked at him thinking he'd gone mad; 'What are you talking about, what is reveting?' It was a good job that it wasn't just me who was ignorant. I had to admit that it was worth a try, so I let him take charge. His first order was for us to go and cut down some small saplings, cut off all the branches and turn them into a stake with point at one end. We carried a lot of equipment with us in the quad, including axes, hammers, picks and shovels which helped us in our task. We put the stakes to one side as he gathered up some wire he had cut off the fence which was around the field. To him it all made perfect sense, but to the rest of us it was getting very puzzling. I looked at him and asked if he was sure what he was doing. 'Don't worry, Sarge', came the reply. 'Just wait, all will be explained'. With that, he called us around him; now he was really taking charge. 'Right you.' he said, pointing to me, 'get the hammer out of the trailer'. So, feeling like a little boy, off I go and get the bloody hammer. When I came back, he then ordered another gunner to hit this stake with the hammer whilst I held it in place. He also told the gunner to make sure he hit the stake and not my hand… Apparently he had been hit before when doing something like this. I later found out that he was a farm labourer. The stakes were placed about two feet apart. He then started to place the branches we had removed from the saplings horizontally between the stakes and banks of the trench. He ordered two more soldiers to get into the trench and start digging deeper, looking to me as though asking what depth I wanted it. I told him about three feet, which I amended to four to be on the safe side. As this was going on, more branches were added until the depth had been achieved. When all was finished he tied wire to the top of each post. He then tied each wire to a smaller stake about two feet from the trench side, tensioning it by hammering the small stake, thereby pulling the long stakes tight against the branches which held the banks. He certainly knew what he was doing. it was a good job he did, and it was to save our lives, as you will read later.

I don't know if you have ever dug in Dutch soil. If you have, you will know that it is very sandy; after all, almost of Holland is reclaimed from the sea. There is a lesson to learn from this story; you are never too young or old to learn from someone else. I have done this all of my life and at ninety-six I am still learning.

At midday on the 17th, we were called to the command post and told that we would see something the likes of which we, or even the generations to come, would never see again in our lives, All the command post officers told us was that at approximately 1300 hours we would see thousands of Airborne and Glider troops landing in front of us. The 101 American Division at the Son bridge and the 82nd Airborne at Eindhoven, Graves and Nijmegen. The British Airborne were to take the bridge at Arnhem. Our job in the 43rd Wessex Infantry Division was to advance and relieve them. We would then travel up what was later known as the 'Hell's highway' and fight our way to Arnhem, where the 1st British Airborne and Gliders had landed 64 miles away - and we were to do this in two days. This was impossible. It took us two days to reach the Graves bridge, and we still had about 50 miles to go. On top of that we were being cut off by the Germans, which in turn meant no supplies could get through. This is famously portrayed in the film 'A Bridge Too Far'.

This was Field Marshal Montgomery's idea; he felt that by capturing the bridges, and in particular the bridge at Arnhem, the allies could cross the Rhine and reach the Zider sea, cutting off the Germans who were retreating on our left flank desperately trying to get back into Germany. By doing this he was sure that the war would be over by Christmas 1944. Eisenhower and General Bradley were doubtful, but still allowed Montgomery to carry on; this was one of his biggest mistakes.

He was told many times, by his intelligence officers showing him photos taken by low flying aircraft and information fed back by the Dutch Resistance, that the Germans were waiting with heavy tanks and fresh troops. But he was not convinced, and believed that the Germans were poorly equipped and that their troops were all old men and young boys. He soon found out that the resistance reports were right, and it took another four months before the Canadians captured Arnhem and reached the German border. All this was told to me soon after the war. I have a very good memory as no doubt you will have noticed whilst reading this book.

Operating from home bases, the Luftwaffe was one to one with the RAF. Montgomery should have known this if had had looked back to when we had been ordered to close up when we were travelling in convoy towards Neerpelt, or perhaps his officers in his command post never thought to tell him. The other indications were that the enemy was resisting the attempts of the 8th and 12th Corps to secure the flanks.

At 1400 hours, the Divisional Artillery opened up a three hundred gun rolling barrage for the breakout of the Irish Guards' tanks. The first nine tanks were destroyed immediately on crossing the Canal and the barrage was repeated to restore the Guards' momentum.

On the 18th, 30 Corps advanced on a six hundred yard front and reached Valkenswaard, well out of artillery range, at around 1900 hours. There was a heavy attack by about fifty or so German bombers on the regimental gun positions, dropping anti-personnel bombs, their machine guns firing tracers most of the night, Tracers were bullets that could seen by the machine gunners to enable them to see where their rounds were falling; we could see them too. The 220 battery suffered the most casualties; Gunners Luck, Davie and Stewardson were killed and five others were wounded. The wounded were evacuated, and most returned after hospital treatment. Sergeant Harold Porter, also of the 477 Battery, was a great friend of mine; unfortunately, he was wounded and died of his wounds early the next morning. I will always miss him; he could make everyone laugh. On one particular evening which I remember well, whilst we were at Broadstairs, England in 1942, all NCOs were called to a meeting in the sergeant's mess by the commanding officer, Major Steel-Perkins. He lectured us on what he felt was lack of discipline. Just after he left and was hardly out of the door, Harold started laughing at himself as he said very loudly 'Who's a naughty boy!' Steele – Perkins heard him, and told Sergeant Major Bert Ramsdon. It was the first time and the only time that I ever saw Bert angry, and he insisted that Harold went to see the CO and apologise, which he did.

During this attack we saw tracers for the first time. There no reason for us to see them, as we were at least three and half miles behind the front line. As we were watching, it looked as though they were coming at us, so we kept dodging them. Silly fools! If they had been fired straight at us, I wouldn't be here now. As it was pointed out to me later on, you never see any bullets except the one that's got your name on it, and then you're dead and it's too late; in which case, I would not be telling you this story.

I was in our second gun position after our landing. I have always been one who keeps on the move when going into action, checking everything was going as I expected, laying the dial sight on the correct line by my No. 3, the No. 2 checking that the breach was working, and Nos. 4, 5 and 6 all dealing with the ammunition. Whilst I was running around supervising all this, I heard what I can only describe as a whistling sound past my ear. I thought little about it, but then there was another, and then another… It was then one of my gunners shouted to me to get down as a sniper was trying to shoot me. I just stood there, staring in disbelief, before the gunner pulled me down. It was reported to the command post, and it was not many minutes before the recce unit came to the rescue. The sniper was in the cornfield. That was a close one, Albert.

MAAS/WAAL CANAL

Slow progress was made, but we continued to support the right flank of 30 Corps. Convoys of supplies continued to pass through with some difficulty; it was reported back that the Guards Armoured Division had linked up with the US 101st and 82nd Airborne at Eindhoven, all the way to Nijmegen.

As I have mentioned Eindhoven, I have another story that I call 'the Lady in Black'. It was when we entered Eindhoven, we were as always bringing up the rear of the column behind the infantry. As a result, we never received the acclaim like they did; girls, boys, men and women would climb onto the vehicles, kissing all of the troops. It certainly had a carnival atmosphere, everyone was so happy by being liberated. I never saw this either in France or Belgium, what with food and wine being given out in large quantities and above all seeing the girls in skirts in all sorts of colours including orange, the colour of Holland. During the occupation by the Germans they were never allowed to show the colour orange but now it was everywhere. I found out later that they had collected the parachutes which were left behind after the landings, the colours relating to the cargo they carried, such as food, ammunition and even light vehicles and guns. They must have collected them within minutes of the landings whist fighting was going on – amazing.

Now back to the Lady in Black. We had entered Eindhoven and come to a stop, waiting to move on. An elderly lady in a long black dress came out and stood in front of me and asked, in perfect English, 'Where do you come from?' I was surprised; I did not know at that time that the Dutch spoke English. I looked at her and asked her what she meant. I explained I had come from the Normandy beach. She then said 'No, I mean where do you come from in England?' Out of the blue, I told her Canterbury, which of course wasn't true. I was aware that there were German spies everywhere, and I no intention of telling her that we'd left Tilbury Docks. Before I could say any more, she excitedly shouted out to her husband 'this gentleman comes from Canterbury!' It turns out that this is where she'd come from, before marrying her husband. What a coincidence! A pity that I never asked her what part she used to live in, before we moved off.

It wasn't until we reached the bridge at that we did any firing. We had set ourselves up with details from the command post and director, when I was given the order to start firing two rounds. We loaded the first round into the breach, and on my command the No. 3 fired. There was a load report and the shell sped off to its target several miles away. The cartridge was ejected and the second round rammed home. Again I gave the order to fire but this time it was different. There was a load bang with a second almost immediately after it. The shell had exploded just outside of the gun, which is known as a 'premature', meaning a shell detonating too soon. This was the first and the only time that it happened to me, thank goodness. Had it exploded inside the breach, I would not be here telling my story.

The 43rd was delayed by one day. Travelling was slow hour after hour, as all vehicle movement was down just one road that was raised above the Dutch polders. By 0300 hours we had moved only forty miles. There was no way we could go forward or turn back. We were unable to get off the narrow road, and if we managed to we would go into the ditch full of water, so we came to a halt and slept for three hours in our vehicles. I remember that we stopped for three days and we were short of rations and water. We were given glasses of milk by the ever-giving Dutch, but we had no breakfast. How much more could the Dutch have given us? They were short of food as well, but they were always so generous throughout the war.

There was so much confusion caused by enemy aircraft and artillery attacks. I don't remember much, it being so far back, but I found out afterwards that we were being cut off, and behind us was a column of some 3000 mixed vehicles, 848 of which were 'A' echelon, which were the lorries carrying ammunition, petrol, food, and everything else to keep an army going. I don't remember much after this, until we got to the Nijmegen bridge and over the other side. Once we'd crossed, we stopped again by a church; I was telling myself we would never make it as we were already one day behind schedule. It was then I heard someone shouting. I couldn't make out what he was saying. Thinking that the Germans had got through our lines, which was the last thing I wanted. I picked up my Sten submachine gun, shaking like a leaf. I'd not shot anyone during the whole of the campaign so far and I wondered if he was going to be my first. Please God, don't make me pull the trigger, I thought. Killing someone had been my greatest fear; someone,who might have had a wife, children, a mother and father. I know they were the enemy, but seeing and killing was not what I joined the artillery for. I know that's what war is all about; you kill them or they kill you. Of course, being three miles behind the front lines I never saw who or how many I killed, and I do not want to know.

Back to the shouting. As it got closer I heard the word 'kaput' repeated time after time. It was a horse and wagon; there was the man sitting very high up on the wagon, shouting ever louder 'kaput, kaput'. I knew what kaput means - dead or no good in German. It was only when he got near that it became apparent that the wagon was full of dead Germansl no wonder he was so excited. He then pulled into the church graveyard. There was a large trench which had been dug and which I'd not noticed before. He backed his wagon up to it and pulled out the bar which held the wagon upright, tipping the whole lot into it, still shouting and laughing 'kaput!' with delight. It has stuck with me ever since.

On the 20th of September, we fired in support of the Guards' Division and the 82nd Airborne but I don't recall any details of our action. All of these dates were supplied by Lt. Douglas Goddard from our regimental history book, with some details of Market Garden. The rest is from my own memory.

On the 23rd we were finally on the move; it was a great to be advancing after three days of waiting and not knowing what was happening. We had only fired one round near Graves bridge, if you exclude the 'premature' detonation. The next time was after crossing the Nijmegen bridge when the tanks and the division managed to advance. We came to a turning off the single road and reached the village of Bemmel, where we then carried on firing for several hours. We then got orders to move on to a new position near Elst, on the banks of the Rhine, and told to dig a gun pit. To me this was a mad idea considering the wet ground; however a gun pit we dug. Orders were orders. Whilst we were digging we heard that orders had been given that the airbourne troops were going to be withdrawn, and that we should be ready at 2300 hours to start firing a box barrage to help them to cross over the Rhine. The plan was for the 4th Dorsets to go over the Rhine and arrange themselves between the river and the enemy, but leave an opening for the airborne to enable them to pull back. At the same time one of our own artillery officers, Zeke Rose, plus two signalers in a Bren Gun Carrier, would go over the river to act as our forward observation post. Zeke was the only OP artillery officer over the other side of the Rhine and as a result he was controlling all of our artillery; some 500 guns, including the mediums and the heavies – the most that any artillery officer in the British Army had ever controlled single-handedly. He was one of our Regiment. How proud we were. Unfortunately Zeke, the two signallers and the driver were killed.

It rained all night and we used our gas capes as best we could to keep dry. They were issued to us in case of a gas attack, which never came – but of course the gun pit filled up with water, and by the time we had finished firing at 0600 hours it was up above our knees. We had been firing intently and only had three rounds of ammunition left when the airborne troopers came back through our gun lines. Only 2000 left out of the 8000 who'd landed on the 17th. It was a pitiful sight. They were looking so tired as they walked through our guns, they looked nothing like british Infantrymen as they marched to the front line. I remember seeing them when they stopped and sat down by the roadside and were given a cup of hot tea. I'm not sure who gave it to them; possibly the Dutch, who were always willing to help in any way they could. Even today, when any veteran visits Holland, their welcome is very sincere, as I have seen so many times.

It was nice to see an article in the Wyvern newsletter by General Tower, a gunner himself, praising the role of the Gunners that night. What more could we say?

From the 24th of September to the 7th October, we remained on what was known as 'the island'. The Germans had broken the banks of the dykes which allowed the water to flow and made a small river to form an island. Although the evacuation of the airborne was completed, ammunition amazingly managed to get through. How this happened I really do not know, as the supply route was sixty miles and was still being cut regularly. Added to that, refugees were pouring down the road in the opposite direction as the fighting continued.

During this time an order signed by Hitler was issued to capture 43rd Division and that it was to be annihilated at all cost. The Germans used to refer to us as 'the yellow devils'.

From the 8th October to the 8th November we withdrew to Groersbeek / Mook Ridge, east of Nijmegen, overlooking the German border and the Reichwald forest, part of the Siegfried line. This was comprised of concrete bunkers holding heavy guns. They were joined with concrete tank traps; these were a pyramid shape with iron bars enclosed in them. No tank could get through, not even the German Tiger Tank. Funnily enough, I do remember that we had a bath when the mobile bath unit arrived. They pumped water from the Maas and Waal rivers and heated it. From what I remember, it wasn't very hot, but all the same it was very welcome after that long journey from Neerpelt.

I also remember there was the talk that General Brian Horrocks gave to the officers and NCOs. He had white hair and a cheerful face, unlike Montgomery. I could have listened to him all day. He gave us a talk on the lessons to be learned from Market Garden. It was printed and issued to everyone there; apparently it was for the benefit of the artillerymen whose hearing might have been affected by the continuous firing of the barrage during the evacuation of the airborne. He pointed out that in the first week the road was only opened for a total of twelve hours. He made a remark about how valuable the work of the Artillery had been in giving fire support to the evacuation of the Airborne Division over the Rhine. He also went on to talk of the failure to capture the bridge. After thinking a while, he looked at us with a straight face. 'No, it was not a failure', he said, 'we may not have acheived our ultimate target, and the war will not be over by Christmas as we had hoped, but at least we have liberated half of Holland and I think we should all be proud of that'. Finally he explained to the other arms, that the gunners had done their 'milk rounds', which meant that the artillery had carried on firing onto the German batteries and destroyed them. He went on to say that if the 43rd had not succeeded, he didn't think there would have been any more of the Fighting Wessex left, and we should be grateful for that. The cheers he got could be heard a mile away, and they were genuine. In my mind, he should have been in Montgomery's place as 21st Army Commander. He was adored by all who were under the 30th Corps Commander.

Between the 8th November and the 6th December we travelled to the Dutch/German border and during that time the 43rd Division were fighting around the Gelsenkirchen, Reeweg, Hamback, and other areas. It was now getting very cold. I'm not sure where I found it, but I acquired a heavy sheet of material, like the sheet that was used to cover haystacks. It came in handy now, as we laid it on the ground behind the gun, and when we were not required three of the gun crew would have a nap. If it was very cold we would pull one half over us and use our kitbag as a pillow. We were the envy of the other gun crews; none of us ever got cold at night or during the day. We always had to have three men on the gun round the clock. Sleep was very important so we would get as much as we could whenever we could, as sometimes we could be up all night. Reading our letters and newspapers, and eating the cakes sent by our families was also very important for us, as were mittens (gloves were no good when on the gun). Letters and parcels could sometimes take weeks before we got them.

Now, going back to Gelsenkirchen. I remember it very well; so many things happened. Firstly we had a 48-hour leave to go to Antwerp; not a very interesting place other than the many red light houses. Many of our men used them. Not me, I hasten to add; I had a wife back home. When I got back to my gun another two went and so on, it gave us a break and it helped with the morale of the regiment, which was very important.

On the 16th December, we handed our position over to another regiment and moved back for a very welcome rest to Beek in Holland, where we enjoyed comfort in churches and delightful houses, and the people gave us the usual Dutch welcome and gratitude. We also got free baths at the nearby coal mine. We soon found out that this rest period was not going to last, and we had move out fast. News came that the Germans had made a breakthrough in the Ardennes in southern Belgium, with the aim of driving through to the north and the river Meuse at Liege and on to Antwerp cutting off the 21st British Army Group from the Americans. This became known as the Battle of the Bulge. The American 101st and 82nd Airborne were preparing to go back to England to brought back up to strength with new men, with the intention of training them ready for the Rhine crossing. Instead, they were sent to the front line at Bastogne where the Germans were advancing fast. At this point, I must mention that it was snowing very heavily and there were low clouds, so no aircraft could fly. This made it easy for the advancing Germans and they surrounded Bastogne with the Airborne trapped in the centre. It was then we moved closer to the action. The Dorsets were sent forward to help the Airborne get out of a very nasty position, and luckily at this time the clouds lifted and aircraft could take off. That was the turning point of the battle of the Ardennes.

    This meant that the preparations being made for the crossing of the Rhine had to be put off. The Commander in Chief, Eisenhower, decided to deploy 30 Corps with Montgomery in charge of thwarting the German's advance to the river Meuse in case they crossed the river. The 43rd was responsible for the left flank, and this is where the regiment was involved. I remember it well; our battery position was in a field near a place called Huy near Liege, and this is where the tarpaulin sheet came in handy again. What luck I'd had in finding it! There was heavy frost, snow and very cold water to wash and shave with. We used our mess tins; however, these could only heat up enough to enable us to wash and shave. We had balaclavas and mittens, many of them were made by Women's Institute members, and also by wives and girlfriends. It was so cold that they were worn day and night. Our troop leader Lt. Johnson (Ginger) had a sleeping bag; he wore also wore this day and night, and in the morning he kept it on whilst washing his face. He had a beard for several weeks afterwards. Beards, incidentally, were normally only allowed with the CO's permission but he got away with it only because we were in action. Our RSM Bill Reeves went berserk, saying 'What in the hell are you doing? It's not a a very good example to the men!'. 'It is cold' was Ginger's reply. Whilst it was still cold, I would walk up to him saying 'How is mummy's boy, is it cold for you my little darling?' When we were in action, anyone above the rank of sergeant would always be friendly and call each other by name, and not worry about rank.

After returning to the gun position the farmer's son came to my gun. He could speak English very well, and he asked me to come to dinner. I had to tell him I was not allowed, but seeing the disappointment on his face I went and spoke to Lt. Johnson and the Battery Sgt. Major Bill Reeves. They both agreed, I could go as the house was nearby and could be reached if we had to move. As I did not drink, I took my bottle of whisky as a present; their eyes nearly shot out of their heads. They hadn't seen Scotch since before the war. It didn't take long before it had all gone. Now here is the funny part of the story… Everything was put on the plate and to my surprise a large spoonful cooked green plums was put into the middle of everything, I was the one whose eyes shot out of my head this time. To me plums were a dessert, not something to go into your dinner. However, it was wonderful – the English should try it.

We had within the regiment, a battery quartermaster, Doug Wainright, who supplied all of the needs of the battery (447). There was also a regimental quartermaster, Bert Norman, who served the needs of the regiment. Unknown to us, Bert had a large quantity of bank pay-in books, which could be used by the men to send cash home instead of leaving it in their regimental account. Let me explain; when in England, we would be paid weekly. When we went abroad, we were first given French francs, (Euros were not in existence) but as there was nothing for any of us to spend our francs on, we wanted to send it home. That way it could either help our wives and families, or go into a bank account so that there would be something saved when the gun troops came home.

However, none of us knew anything about this, but the RQMS together with the BQM kept them for themselves. When the town of

Gelsenkirchen was taken, there was a large quantity of sugar found in a store building; this was something that Bert and Doug could not resist. They found a buyer in Holland, just over the border from Germany. It was easy to transport from Gelsenkirchen, but they had the problem of how to get the money to England.

This where Doug came in handy. He was the only one who came into contact with the gun troops, and this provided them with the opening they needed. They were a crafty lot. In February 1945 we were all given a pass home for ten days leave, and it was Doug's job to bring any supplies needed by the battery in the field, which he did. This was the opportunity they were waiting for. It was Doug's job, whenever anything was wanted (normally twice a week), to visit the guns. Whilst there, he would ask who was going on leave to Swindon where they had families. Most of our men came from there, so it was easy to find someone who would take a letter home to his family… But, in fact, it was the money they had received from the sugar sale, and with it a letter telling the recipient to bank it.

We now understood why he brought in a three ton truck, when a thirty hundred weight one was all that was needed. He would go from the gun position to get the sugar and take it to Holland, where he would collect the money in Dutch guilders, then give it to Bert, who would put it in the envelope with the letter which then Doug would hand to the person who was going home on leave. I always left my money in the regimental account, and I took it when I went on leave at the end of February, and gave it to Ann who was saving up to buy furniture, crockery, and clothes for our first baby Roger, who was born on the first of June 1946. To the readers that must sound odd, but when you read my life story you will understand.

At that time, the Division was about to attack the Reichwald forest, which I missed. Not really! It was good to be home for the first time since we'd gone to Normandy, and seeing Ann and all of her family, including my Mum, Dad, and sister Dolly. Funnily, I kept reading the papers hoping to see where the regiment might have got to, but of course the papers were not allowed to mention any movements of any of the forces without permission.

When I got back to my gun position, I was surprised we how far we had advanced into Germany; by March 1945 we were on the banks of the Rhine. We had a period of rest, but each gun had to supply two men each day to work with the Pioneer Company. We knew nothing of the work being carried out; it was only when they returned did we find out. My two gunners told us that their job was to lay a foundation of concrete. Next to it was concrete already laid, but during the night (only the Engineers and the Pioneers) had laid metal poles in a sloping position. Nobody else knew what it was all about. The same thing happened the following night, and so on, until five of the six foundations were ready. The next day two more gunners went to finish off the last foundation; it was then that large barrels of oil had been placed into position all along the bank of the Rhine. Again, this hadhad happened at night, the only difference being that there was also a large generator, with cables leading from it to these sloping poles. At about 0900 hours, the oil barrels were set alight. We could see the smoke from our gun positions and it started to make sense… The smoke was screening everything that was going on with the generator, the cables and the sloping poles from the enemy. All was about to be revealed. It was all to do with rockets. We had only previously seen Russians and battleships use rockets; never before by the Allies on the battlefield. Today they are used in any conflict where needed, even for the laying of mines.

In March, we moved close to the banks of the Rhine, and the following day in the early hours of the morning all of our artillery opened up a barrage lasting half an hour. Then the glider borne troops and Airborne troops dropped over the Rhine. At the same time, the Engineers started building a pontoon bridge which would allow light vehicles including our quad, gun and limber. Now, if you have never driven over a pontoon bridge you might not know that you need a very clear head, especially when the you are driving a limber attached to the quad, the gun attached to the limber. You have two movements, plus the gun swaying side to side and there are only twelve inches spare when crossing. I watched the number one gun go over and saw the movement of the pontoon bridge as it reacted to the weight of the whole unit travel across it. My driver and I felt sick and scared as we got our quad into position and slowly started to cross to the other side. The first gun was half way when it was our turn to follow. I remember looking down at my driver, Ron Smith. He was white as a sheet and trembling, and I was no better. We were brought to our senses by an engineer shouting 'For Christ's sake get a bloody move on!' As you already know, being the Number One in the gun team it was my job to stand up through the hole in the roof of the quad at all times, and I was looking down at the fast flowing Rhine from my high perch. Although the bridge is held in position by steel hawsers, one on either side, they still did not stop the bridge moving out of line, so there was a slight curve in the bridge cause by the flow of water, which really didn't help the situation one little bit. We moved very slowly. I glanced down at the driver and he was holding onto the steering wheel as tight as he could and trembling. I kept telling him to watch the wheels, and I was trying calm him down, telling him not to worry as he had at least 6 inches to spare either side. I realise now that this was the last thing he wanted hear. We got less than half way and it seem to us that the bridge was moving more. Poor old Smithy nearly stopped. It was at that point that I shouted loudly at him to get moving and gave him a kick. He put his foot hard down on the accelerator, and I nearly shot out of the top! We got to the other side much quicker than expected. After a few minutes to calm down on terra firma, we moved forward, and I remember both of us saying at the same time that we hoped we'd never have do that again.

One of the most puzzling things was that I thought we were in Germany, but the names were in Dutch. How could this be? It was only later that I understood that over the other side of the river was Holland, and this small part was also Holland, divided by the Arnhem bridge. No wonder that if it had been captured, it would have shortened the war.

Being so far back behind the infantry, we never saw any dead British soldiers lying in the fields; they were always picked up and buried in small graves where they had fallen, with a small wooden cross or their rifle upside down with the tin helmet on the top. All of us carried two small discs around our necks with name, rank and number on, including blood type and religion. My service number was 890390. One disc was kept by the burial party, the other was sent home to the next of kin together with all of their belongings, pay book etc. This was done by an officer from the Ministry of War. Beforehand, a telegram of condolence was sent as quickly as possible to the nearest relative.

The Germans were in full retreat, with nowhere else to go but into Germany, and they intended to fight for Hitler and the Fatherland. Fight they did, but in their hearts they knew it was pointless.

Our next position was near Oldenburg, Germany. As I said early on, I was always number two gun, but this time I was ordered to the number one position. This puzzled me and Pete Holloway, who had always been number one gun. What on earth was going on? Anyway, orders were orders so off I went. Now, our normal positions were in a staggered formation which means one gun in front, second to the rear, third in front and fourth to the rear. The gun positions were chosen by the second in command; in our case Major Heathcoat. Wherever possible we were situated below a sloping hill, as this helped us hide from the enemy by being behind a slope where they could not see us, unless they climbed up a tree or building to give them extra height. However, this time the number one gun, me, was placed on top of the hill. This was unusual, and there were many trees about a thousand yards in front. I always made my gunners dig a slit trench as soon as possible; as I explained to them, it might save their lives as it had done at Neerpelt.

When the gun had been prepared my gun layer, Ken Radford, looked around and said 'Look Sarge, we're in a tank attack position!' My God, so we were., As I've just described we were normally staggered; however, this time we were in off centre line, which meant that each gun had a clear view of any tanks coming from the front and either flank, without firing and hitting each other gun. It sounds very complicated but it's just common sense. We had not been in action very long before I was being hit by German air burst shells; me and two of my gunners were on the gun. We had not been called to action stations, so the other three were resting. The shrapnel was falling like rain hitting our helmets, the gun and the grass smoldering as though it was on fire because of the hot metal. The only place that the enemy could have had an observer who'd seen me was up one of those trees. This kept on for nearly ten minutes, and got more intense. I pressed the button on the Tannoy to call the command post. Sergeant Major Bert Ramsdon answered, and I asked him what in the hell was going on. Were they trying to get me killed? Were they expecting a tank attack? I told them that I thought there might be an observer in the trees. He told me not to worry, and that they were going to find another position in the rear, out of sight of prying eyes.

At that moment the grub wagon came up to the rear of the command post. We only send three men at a time, leaving the other three on the gun just in case an order comes through. I decided to go in the second group to get some grub. I started talking to Bert whilst eating my grub (we never used the word food in the field), telling him to get a bloody move on with the reposition, otherwise we would all be killed.

'Alright', he said, 'don't get your knickers in a twist! I'm sorry'. At that moment the air bursting stopped. I thought they may have run out of ammunition. No such luck. At the same time I looked across the other side of the field and I couldn't believe what I was seeing. It was infantrymen, coming up slowly with their rifles at the ready. I asked Bert if I was seeing things, and what the troops were doing.

'Oh, don't worry', he replied, 'your gun is the only thing which is holding the Germans up'. 'Do you mean to say I'm in the front line?'

'Yes, and I think you should get a medal'. 'Bugger the medal', I replied. 'Get us out of here, and bloody quick!'

Bert was as larger than life man; not only that, he was actually a large man. He rode a 250 BSA motorcycle. It always gave us a laugh riding behind him, seeing his fat backside and huge body sitting on this small motorbike. If Bert decided not to ride his motorbike, he would get into the back of the wireless truck with the troop leader's assistant, Bombardier Beach. Now, for those of you who do not know the size of the wireless truck, you would probably think that sounds fine…, But the truck is only large enough for the wireless and its operator, the troop leader and driver, and the kit for the three of them. As I've said, Bert was a large person and all he could was to sit on the tailboard. I was watching him climb aboard; it was so funny, as he was just about blocking out any daylight in the truck. It also looked like that at any minute the truck would tip up backwards with the weight of Bert sat on the back. The truck had only just started to move when an 88 shell landed to the right of the truck. This was known as a marker. The next one landed right behind the truck, killing both Bert and the Bombardier. I was totally stunned. I had only been speaking to him a minute before, and now he was dead. I have to admit, I cried. Not only was he a good BSM, but he was also a great friend, and even today whilst writing this I can feel the tears running down my face. Unfortunately the timing could not have been worse. April 3rd 1945, a little over a month before the war finished on the 8th May. It took a long time for our men to find the parts of the bodies. This is something none of the gunners had ever done; it was usually done by the medical unit, but as we were going to move on in the evening, somebody had to do it. To our astonishment the regimental padre came within an hour and held a service. Apparently he knew we were in shock at the sudden deaths of these two men, and he felt it would help us to get over it. It certainly did. We left Oldenburg that evening.

In the meantime, the Yeomanry Forester Tanks, followed by our infantry and then us, had advanced and captured Ensharde with very little fighting. Our next objective was Hengelo, where heavy fighting took place with casualties on both sides. It took until the 5th before it was finally captured. We stopped for eight days in Hengelo for a well deserved rest, the battery was billeted and was warmly welcomed in local houses. There were three in ours, Sgt. Ted Ford, Dickenson and myself, there was only one middle-aged lady who would have been about 45 in the house and not very good looking. In actual fact, she look more like a witch – she only needed a broom stick to complete the picture! We had very little to do except maintain the gun, limber and vehicle. The spare evenings were spent in the pub, having had a shower at the baths in a local factory.

Our next objective, on the 13th April, was the town of Bremen not far from the harbour of Bremen-haven. At about midday on the 8th May, 1945 we were in action near Bremen. We had been there for two days without firing a shot. We often wait two or three days when the infantry and tanks go to their starting point before we start a barrage; however, this time there was a funny message over the tannoy…

'Cease firing and limber up', which means we were to move to another position. This was followed by another three words which I had never heard before when in action. 'It's all over'. Now that was puzzling, so I pressed the talk button and the command post officer replied.

'Yes? What do want number two?'

'What do you mean, sir?'

'Well', came the reply 'the bloody war is over!'

That was the biggest surprise for all of us. During the whole campaign we never knew what was going on. We didn't know that Hitler had shot himself in April, or that the Russians were in Berlin; but we were always going forward, so we knew that Jerry was beaten.

THE ANGER

Getting my gun out of action proved to be very difficult, to put it mildly. The quad came up and we hooked the limber and gun to it and started to move, but unfortunately the gun and quad got stuck. Unknown to me, we were in a wet spot, which made me swear as we, the battery, had captured a German 30 cwt. wagon of spirits, and this was going to be used for a party when the war was over. However, going back to my gun position the only way to get out of this situation was to winch the quad, limber, and gun, which is a very slow process. First you have to unhitch the limber and the gun from the quad. With that done, you then winch the quad out first by the using the cable winch in the rear of the quad, passing it under the quad before pulling it to the front. You also have what is known as a winch wheel, which is placed in front of the quad and is held in position by steel pins. I know it sounds very complicated, but it's easy when you have been trained to do it. The driver then fixes the cable to the front of the quad. The winch gear is then put into four wheel drive, and the quad then pulls itself out. Then the procedure is reversed and the limber and gun is pulled out using the quad's winch. It took two hours before we were on solid ground. By this time, the other three guns were out of action and away, and all we had was a cup of cold tea. We got on the road but did not know which way to go to find the rest of the battery. Were we to turn right or left? Nobody had bothered to tell me which way to go and I had no map reference, so was in limbo. It was then that the battery came back, which was another puzzle. It was not until Sgt. Major Reeves explained that the Germans would not surrender, so they had been given an ultimatum. Either they laid down their arms within half an hour, or we would shell them and they would have to take the consequences of their actions. They soon made up their mind and surrendered.

That was it. The war was at an end, and with it all the unnecessary killing due to the fanatical Nazi regime over the six years of the conflict.

We eventually got back to our parking area, only to find that the officers had pinched all of our spirits. It had been our intention to hold a sergeant's mess party at the end of the war. This party was now denied to us, which mad all of us angry. To our horror, we also found out that the quartermaster had a store of Brasso and Blanko in his wagon. Now we had to get back to being a peacetime army and clean ourselves up. Bollocks. The reason for this was that we were going into Germany as the victors, passing through the lines of German prisoners. When an enemy has been defeated in war, they are made to lay down their arms, take off their helmets and undo their collars. In other words they are in disgrace. It would also cement in their minds that they had let down Hitler and the Nazi party. This of course is what the Allies went to war over in the first place, to destroy that evil regime. From my point of view it was very scary, and as I stood out of the quad I was very nervous. I know that if I saw any of them making any attempt to have a go at me, I would have shot them.

We now become the British Army of Occupation Rhine, BAOR, and we were informed that we must not fraternize with any Germans. This proved to be a fruitless operation, for in the end we were having to protect the Germans from displaced personnel; those who had been taken from all over Europe and put into forced labour camps, such as the one at Belsen.

We now come to another happy time. We made our way to a place called Bomlitz near Fallingbostle, also near the Belsen concentration camp. It was at Bomlitz that we had our first proper billets, with proper beds, for the very first time since the start of the war in 1939. We had white sheets and blankets, flushing toilets, running water and gardens. It was at Bomlitz that some of our division entered the concentration camp, including our medical officer, and helped to organize the burying of the dead. Officers and soldiers were sent out to round up German civilians and make them help with burying all the bodies. All Germans either knew or did not want to know that these concentration camps existed. Of course they knew, but were afraid of the Gestapo who would have had them shot for admitting they did exist.

This is where the unexpected duty of looking after the Germans came to the fore. One day in June 1945, when I was in charge of a guard duty some distance from Bomlitz, a German girl came rushing into the guard house, screaming 'Come quickly!' She could speak good English, as could many Germans. Apparently, a displaced person, a Pole, was stealing food and goods from the farmhouse. The Pole had no gun, nor did any Germans other than farmers who were allowed to keep a shotgun for foxes, rabbits and deer. I followed the girl to to the farm on a bicycle, but the man had gone. The same thing happened the next day, and so I stayed for the night at the farm, sleeping in a chair with my Sten gun by my side; but nothing happened. The Pole must have been watching me return to the farm and not come back. He must have been laid up somewhere, from where he could see the coming and goings of the farm. It did not occur to me that he was laying in the corn.

Although the war had finished on the 8th May 1945, my time in the army did not. I was to stay in the army until mid-February 1946, but I feel I must bring it to a conclusion with the end of my story.

In August 1945, mw and a friend of mine called Ted Ford were posted back to the Royal Artillery Barracks in Woolwich, London and apparently we were to go to the Far East to fight in the war against Japan. We felt this was unfair having fought in Western Europe; however, when we got to the port at Ostend, the Americans had dropped their first atom bomb in the hope this would put an end to the war. It didn't have the desired effect, so a second bomb was dropped and within two days the Japanese capitulated. Although it was heavily criticized by the general public and the media, it undoubtedly saved many American, British and Commonwealth servicemen's lives.

When Ted and I reached England at the end of August, we had yellow fever innoculations and given ten days leave, after which we went back to the depot and were informed that we would not be going to the Far East, but instead to the Middle East.

It was 1939 when I joined the 112 Royal Artillery Field Regiment, Territorials. I was nineteen, and was called up on the first of September. War was declared against Germany on the third. You have to remember I was just a country lad and still very much a boy who had had very little excitement in his life, but I can assure you it did not take me long to become a man. More so, when you see your own friends die in front of you. It did not take long before the hatred felt for all this senseless killing, that had been brought on by some mad man and his decision to murder thousands of people just because of their religion or for failing to accept the power of his Nazi Party (which needed to have complete power over all the countries they occupied), drove me and many of my friends to fight as hard as possible to liberate these countries.

It took me and my brothers in arms to do this until the invasion of France in June 1944, and then another ten months to finally defeat Nazism. How sweet a victory it was, seeing all those Nazi soldiers and SS officers hanging their heads in shame, having let their Führer down. It made me feel wonderful that I paid a part in this victory on May 8th 1945.

It was then we started sailing towards the Middle East. I need to explain that none of us, some three thousand men, had ever travelled by sea; perhaps only in the English Channel before, and here we were going through Gibraltar, Malta, Taranto (in Italy) and into Alexander Port and on to Port Said, Egypt. From there it was up the Suez Canal to Suez and on to Cairo. From Cairo we went to Heliopolis and on to Almaza, to the BDRA (Base Depot of the Royal Artillery). It was there that we had two options; we could either go to Palestine or become prison warders in Nicosia. After two weeks' training in self defence, me and Ted had decided. I went to Nicosia, and Ted went to Famagusta.

I had a wonderful billet with a drinks bar, and all mod cons like we'd had at Bomlitz in Germany. My duty started at 0600 hours the morning after I arrived, in November 1945. On going on parade line up, the RSM made his inspection, making sure we were looking tidy and so on. He then handed me a truncheon. The truncheon is a heavy stick, fitted with a leather strap. When you use it the strap is slipped over your wrist to keep it in position. I had never even seen or held such a weapon before. When asking the RSM what I was to do with it, he informed me it was for hitting the SUS (Soldiers Under Sentence) with. Hearing this with astonishment, I pointed out that being a sergeant I had been charge of men for over six years and at no time had I ever hit my men. We worked together throughout the war side by side, and as such we made decisions together; there had been many times when one of my gunners would know more than me about how to tackle situations I was unsure in. The RSM's reply was, 'You were in the war, but you will do as I say'. I replied that I would not. He then asked if that meant I would refuse to obey his order, and I replied that it did. Instantly he put me on a charge, which meant I could be court martialled and reduced to the rank of gunner.

When joining as a wartime warder, you had to sign the Official Secrets Act – so you could be shot as a traitor. The RSM announced that I was on a charge, and I would up in front of the commanding officer as soon as he came in that morning. When the CO arrived, the RSM shouted 'Attention, quick march!'. We went in front of the CO and I was called to attention. The RSM then read out the charge.

'When Sergeant Figg was given the truncheon and he asked what he had to with it, I told him it was to protect him from any attack from prisoners. He replied that he had no intention of doing such a thing, and he also remarked that he had been a sergeant since 1941, had been in action during the Normandy landings, and that in all of his time in the forces he had never hit his men and that he has no intention of starting now. I therefore placed him on a charge for refusing to obey an order, sir'.

The funny thing was that whilst the RSM was reading out the charge, the CO never once looked up but carried on writing. He told the sergeant major that he could carry on with his work and that he would see to Sergeant Figg. The RSM stood there waiting to find out what sentence he would give me, but still without looking, the CO repeated 'Carry on, sergeant major!' The poor old RSM went red in the face, obviously angry at being dismissed in such a way.

It wasn't until he had gone that the CO looked up at me with a great big grin.

'Hello Figgy, what in the hell are you doing here?' I must admit I was taken aback, not having ever been spoken to like that by any officers, let alone the CO.

He carried on. 'Don't you remember me? No? well I was in the 112 Field Regiment 447 Battery when you were made Sergeant in Sandwich, 1941. Major Steele-Perkins was our Battery Commander. You don't want this job, do you?'

'No not really', I replied, 'I'm only here until my discharge date comes up, then I want to get to hell out and back home to my wife'.

With that he said 'I have got just the right job for you, how would you like to be the Sergeant Mess caterer? The only thing I insist on, is that I have bottle of whisky every week, which you will be able to get from the Naffi store, and also a couple of watches'.

'That is fine,' I said, 'but I didn't know that the Naffi sold watches.'

His reply was 'go into Nicosia, you will find many Turkish and Cypriots who sell them on the black market at a reasonable price. You just have to haggle with them until you feel you've got the best price possible, but you have to careful not to be seen trading with them as it is illegal'. This went on until I received my discharge date, which was in February 1946, and then it was home to married life.

That was the end of my army days, which I was very sorry to leave; there would not be enough excitement now the war was over, and I still miss the camaraderie, even today, at the age of 95.

HOME TO MARRIED LIFE

My army life had now come to an end, and civilian life started again. In six-and-a-half years, I'd gone from a boy of nineteen to a man of twenty-six years old, with a wife and a baby on the way.

Our first home was with Anne's family at Upper Dully Cottages, Bapchild, Nr Sittingbourne, Kent. Opposite stood Scuddington Manor, known during the war as Wood Street House and which was also our Regimental Headquarters.

Anne had three sisters, Edwina, Kathleen and Evelyn, and along with her Mother Winifred and father Ted. There wasn't much room in a house with only three bedrooms. Ted was a shepherd for a local farmer called Doubleday.

Living with Anne's family was not ideal, but at least we had a roof over our heads; you have to remember that houses were in short supply as so many had been destroyed during the war. None were built during wartime, and with so many men of my age getting married between 1939 and 1946, it took a year or so before the prefabs we were promised were ready.

My first priority was to get a job. As I was working as a private gardener before the war, it seemed only natural that I should do the same thing, but unfortunately, very few people in the area could afford to pay for a gardener, so I had to look in another direction. I wanted my working life to be outside, and luckily a job came my way through my sister in law Edwina's boyfriend, Ken Kinsella. He worked for a local farmer called Mr French on Batteries Farm, which was close by in Lynsted, so it was ideal.

Ken told me there was a job going with Ken French, one of Mr French's sons who had just started a new venture into market gardening. He was using cloches, which were a new idea.. They were like miniature greenhouses which could be moved around and placed over crops like lettuces, tomatoes and radishes' etc. They produced the crops earlier by two to three weeks as they encouraged growth and protected the vegetables from the frost so they were available before the unprotected crops.

I was fortunately given the job, and it was only a matter of minutes by cycle, so I had no travel problems. My wages were £4.5s.0d a week – that was quite good at that time – I was only getting £1.2s.0d, at nineteen, when the war started, in 1939. I know it sounds like a pittance today, but you have to remember everything was much cheaper, and we were still rationed, with some food being in short supply.

[Market Garden]

Washing machines, fridges and televisions were beyond the reach of the working class. Very few people had a car, and horses were still in use on the farms, but tractors were gradually taking over. Money went a little further but of course there was never enough! The same can be said today.

Before I go any further I must also give credit to Anne and her hard work.

When we got married in 1942, she was working in the Land Army for Mr Hales at Newington. She saved nearly all her money to buy furniture and household items like pots and pans. She also rented a house in Frederick Street, Sittingbourne, where we could be together on our own, at weekends, when I was off duty. No matter where I was stationed, such as Broadstairs, Margate and Sandwich, I would get to her by train. Early in 1943, Anne went for training to be a nurse at Bromley Hospital, going onto Willeborough Ashford, and finally to St Marys Hospital, Eastbourne, until early 1944. With her working and saving, by the time war had finished, she had made a home for us including clothes for the baby.

I will be forever grateful to her for her hard work and support. At times, I have to be honest, I was not the easiest of people to live with, and most of my time was taken up with work mostly seven days a week. In my eyes, it was purely for my family, but at times I lost sight of the company of my wife and children. Hindsight is always a wonderful observation if only you could do something about it!

Anne also did her part, working in the fields and well as in the evenings whenever possible, so, at times, it was only natural that she felt neglected; she had four children to look after as well as me working all the hours God sent.

But, getting back to my first job at Ken French's market garden. I think it was sometime in March, 1946 when I started. I had one month's holiday, which the Army had paid for, and a £100 gratuity, which we kept for when the baby was born.

Roger Edward was born on 1st June 1946 and coincidentally, my sister, Dolly, had a daughter June, on the same day.

The weekend after Roger was born, on the Sunday, Anne's father Ted asked me if I would like to go to the pub with him. He liked a pint, so off I went to the Black Lion public house at Lynsted, taking the baby with me. After I met Anne I was never a drinker. A small brown ale was enough for me (I think I had sufficient during my life in the army). We were in the small private bar and a white-haired gentleman came in and acknowledged Ted, also asking at the same time 'who is this you have with you'? 'Oh, this is my son-in-law, he has just come out of the Army.' The gentleman's name was Mr Comyn Ching, and he lived in a large house called Aymers that was situated on the edge of a country lane that was the start of Lynsted.

Mr Ching started asking me questions; what Regiment was I in? The Royal Artillery, I told him. He told me he knew several officers of the Royal Artillery who were stationed at Woodstreet House. 'That's where I was billeted during the war', I replied, 'what were their names?' He said he could remember one called Captain Calderwood, who used to like his drink. 'Yes, I knew him', I replied, and told him that he was our Battery Captain. I also mentioned Major Steele Perkins who was our CO – Mr Ching had met him as well. The conversation carried on for a while and then, all of a sudden, he asked me what I intended to do for a living. I told him I was into private gardening before the war, but was now working for Mr French. He asked me if that was what I intended to do all my life, 'No', I said, 'I would like to have a market garden of my own'. Out of the blue, he told me to find a piece of land and then to go to see and him. I was rather taken aback. I did not know the man or his financial means. As we were walking back home, Ted started telling me just who he was. 'You want to keep in with him, he's a very wealthy man and owns a large factory in London making locks, brass fittings and ironmongery. (You can go to the website comynching.com to find out more).

I now return to where we were living at Upper Dully. We were not happy having to live with Anne's parents; we wanted a place of our own. In August, I was approached by two other ex-service men, asking if we would be able to squat or take over Scuddington Manor, the large house just above where we were living.

I went up there one Sunday morning to look and see if it would be easy to get into, and lo and behold a back door was unlocked. It was important not to break in otherwise, we could have been arrested. So I went back and told the other two that we should move in the following weekend, before anyone else did – and told them to keep quiet about it and not mention it to anyone. Unfortunately, somebody got to hear about it. On the Friday before we were going to move in, the news came out in the local paper that squatters were going to occupy Scuddington Manor, and the police were going to stand guard. That upset all of our plans!

Now before I continue, I should explain that squatting was going on all over the country. Houses that were taken by the government for billets during the war were still empty and most of us young married men, just back from fighting a bloody war, were not going to sit back and be walked over by the government, by councils, or by any officials. They had to take notice of us! No more of the pre-war attitude, sir this and master that; we intended to make sure we were all treated as equal. They were no better than us, and we were no better than them. The reason Churchill was not re-elected after the war was due to us all remembering the Conservatives' way of keeping the working class under the thumb.

Labour got into power in 1945, with a large majority, partly due to the Forces vote. That set the agenda to improve the standard of living. Although I have always since voted Conservative, I have also always regarded myself of a bit of a rebel and opinionated. My experience in the Army and the war made me speak up and stand up for myself. I was not alone; after all, we were the product of our life experiences.

It was not long afterwards that I thought of another place that perhaps we could make a home of our own; not ideal, but I felt it was worth a go. During the war, the Government built what were know as Nissen huts; these were round-topped, galvanized steel buildings set in the grounds of large houses. One such place to have these was Sharsted Court, near Doddington. The three of us went and inspected them, and found that three of them could be made habitable by stripping the other ones, using doors and such to divide the huts into three rooms; a bedroom, a dining/sitting room and a kitchen. Waterworks and toilets were still intact, but outside! There was a large stove in the centre, with the chimney going straight up through the roof, and we would use the surplus wood to keep it going.

Anne was not keen on it, but I promised her I would work and make it comfortable. We moved in during the next weekend, September/October 1946. All three of us helped each other, and by the next weekend we had the rooms divided. I brought some linoleum and covered the floor. Anne made the curtains and with all the furniture she had bought during the war (second hand was all that was available), we called it home. Anne was very happy that we were on our own, and although I had to cycle further for work and take sandwiches with me, I did not mind, it was our own home. The problem of getting water in was overcome by bringing in buckets full last thing at night, before the frost came. I even registered our address for any mail as No. 3 Nissen Hut, Sharsted Court. We eventually got news that our prefab bungalow would be ready in the summer of 1947, and would be situated in Frognal Lane, Teynham.

The winter of 46/47 was the worst since 39/40; deep snow and bitter cold which did not help. The building, as it was made of metal, attracted the frost inside so we were going to bed early to keep warm. We only had a paraffin cooker and lamp. It sounds primitive now, but don't forget that this was what most people had before the war. My mother never had electricity or gas, not until 1944.

We had been in the Nissen hut for two weeks. On the Saturday afternoon, there was a knock on the door; standing outside was a man announcing himself as the Chief Engineer, Mr Randerson from Swale Council, with an eviction order in his hand. He stated emphatically that we had to leave the hut at once; as you can imagine this raised my blood pressure. I quickly collected the other two men and we surrounded Mr Randerson without saying a word. We would have looked very menacing to him and not surprisingly he looked very nervous in return, unsure of what we were going to do. I can see him now, saying 'I don't want any trouble I am only doing my job.'

All three of us started shouting at him; 'Doing your job!' What the hell do you think we've been doing for the last six years, certainly not for you or anyone else to start dictating to us, so get the hell out of here before we frog march you down the road. He did not know what frog marching was, so I showed him; holding his coat collar and the seat of his trousers, I lifted him off the ground and started walking him down the road with his toes just touching the tarmac. After the demonstration I let go, and he ran down the road shouting 'I'm going to call the police!'

Next Sunday came another knock on the door, and standing there was this tall man whose face I knew immediately. Bill Hutchinson had been a Sergeant with me in the same regiment, and it transpired he had joined the police force in Faversham CID after the war. He saw my name on the list in his office, and as it was slightly unusual and thought it could be me, he thought it might be fun to come first hand to read out the charge that I had manhandled Mr Randerson and had stolen material from the site, such as doors and timber. We had a cup of tea, and as he was leaving mentioned there would be no charge to answer, as everything was still on-site; nothing had been stolen. As for the manhandling charge, it was his word against three and Randerson could prove no injuries.

The news got into the national papers that more ex-servicemen were occupying empty houses and in some cases Nissen huts. Within three weeks, all local councils were instructed to make all habitable Nissen huts fit to live in by laying on water and electricity and providing bathroom/toilet. A small charge would have to made for rent, but it certainly made things more pleasant. We remained there until mid-summer, when our prefab was ready.

The prefab, once built, was situated adjacent to Frognal Lane and behind The Fox public house. To the rear was a piece of land which belonged to a Mrs Akins. Before the war it was a fruit tree nursery belonging to her father, but now was overgrown and not being used. You will hear about this later on.

Our new prefab bungalow was wonderful, although it could be cold on winter nights, and sometimes the curtains would freeze against the steel windows… But it was our castle until 1953; we had had three children by then. Roger was born in the June of 1946, Royston in November the following year and then Annette a few years later.

Soon after we moved in, I started looking at this piece of ground opposite our back door. As as I said previously, it was in very bad condition, overgrown with old fruit trees. One Saturday, Mrs Akins came walking on the ground, and I approached her and asked if I could rent or buy a piece of the land for a vegetable garden. Her reply was 'I don't think you could afford it', which instantly made me mad. She didn't know what money I had, or how I could fund it. I said, 'Tell me how much you want for it' '£625', was her reply, with a silly look on her face as if to to say 'you would never be able to afford it'. However, a small piece of it had been sold to the owners of The Fox pub, with the idea of building a new pub. This did not happen, and the land was eventually sold for housing.

I contacted Mr Ching and told him about the ground. He came to see it, but was not very impressed due to the amount of work that had to be done to get it into a cultivated condition. I managed to convince him that I could do it. This was in the autumn of 1947. Mr Ching took me to the Midland Bank in Sittingbourne to meet the bank manager, Mr Wyatt, and arranged a bank loan of £625 to buy the ground and a further £200 to be put into a bank account in my name. To me it was as though I had Father Christmas all to myself.

I still worked for Ken French's market garden during the day. Every evening, Saturday and Sunday I spent digging out the old trees and cleaning the ground, even to the point of using a hurricane lamp to see, with snow sometimes over twelve inches deep. I carried on doing this until it was completed in February 1948. I then invited Mr Ching to come and see what I had achieved. I will always remember the look of total amazement on his face when he saw the transformation from when he first saw it.

Without hesitation he gave me a further £300 to buy a machine known as an iron house, a single furrow plough, to prepare the ground, and to to buy manure to make the soil more productive. Without asking Mr Ching for more money, I managed to find enough to buy a rotavator. It was not a good one, but it did the job of making a fine tild to the soil which was needed before I could plant and place cloches over them. It was then Mr Ching decided to give me a further £1,500 to buy 3000 cloches.

It was at this time I met with a gentleman called Mr Chase, the gentleman who in fact invented the Chase Cloche. His factory in Chertsey, Surrey housed a large demonstration of a market garden. We become very good friends, and when buying all of 3000 cloches he gave me a large greenhouse, with the proviso that I let him use my site as a demonstrator once a year for his potential customers. I remember that on the first occasion for one of these demonstrations, the whole of Teynham High Street was jammed packed with cars, and the police had to be called to direct the traffic to the side of the roads. I got a good telling off by the police for not informing them before hand what was going to happen. Unfortunately, being the first time, I had no idea that there would be so many people coming. I must admit that I felt quite a celebrity!

However, I must go back to when I ordered the cloches. I was still working for Ken French when the large boxes containing the glass and fittings arrived at Teynham railway station. Ken French saw them and immediately gave me the sack, saying he could not have people working for him that were in competition.

I could understand that, but there I was out of a job. Again, Mr Ching came to my aid by giving me another £500. This gave me the time to erect all the cloches, place them on the ground in readiness to plant them up with lettuces, tomatoes and radishes etc.

The cloches were laid out in two rows, side by side, giving a width of planting approximately forty-four inches and a path of twenty-four inches left between the next two rows. This would allow one to walk between to maintain the plants. I had the water laid on and to save money I had it fastened to the wall running down the site, with a tap every thirty feet. I then brought irrigation pipe lines, which were made of rubber about half an inch in diameter with small nozzles, which, when connected to the mains water supply, would water the plants when laid under the cloches.

It was now September, and I had already planted the lettuce seeds that produced the plants for planting under the cloches, six to a cloche; a total of 9000. This planted 1500 cloches and the remainder 1500 cloches were left until early spring 1949 for tomatoes, runner beans and cucumbers.

It was now October, and money was running short. I did not feel that I could accept any more money from Mr Ching, so I had to look around for a job to last until the lettuce crop could be harvested. It was then that Ted, Anne's father, came to my rescue. At this time of the year, chestnut trees were being cut down to be made into pile fencing, and Ted had been doing this for the last two years for a Mr Nye. He suggested that he could show me what to do and he would get Mr Nye to let me have a section of wood of my own, and that he would keep an eye on me to make sure it was done in the correct way. It had to be cut in such a way that allowed the rainwater to run off the stock;

a reverse V shape. My father-in-law told me I would get paid £1 per 100 large poles, and £1.5s.0d per 100 small poles. To cut all branches off each pole, the largest branches I would have to tie up in bundles of ten, and the smaller branches in bundles of twenty; these would be used for runner beans and peas. I could sell these myself and keep the money and could earn an extra £1 per week, all the other brushwood had to be burnt. Ted gave me an axe and a billhook and showed me how to sharpen them, which was very important. He spent half a day with me and then left me on my own.

I tried to earn at least £5 a week; to do this I had to cycle about eight miles either way, taking sandwiches and a flask of tea. I would start at six in the morning and got home at six in the evening, six days a week. This went on until the end of March, when cutting had to stop to allow new growth to start on the stock root.

Ted would go to Mr Nye's house to collect the money every Friday night, and he would bring the money to me at our bungalow. This went on for two months, until Mr Nye came to the wood and saw me. He asked why did I not collect my own money and suggested that I should do this from now on but not giving the reason why.

So the following Friday I went to his house at Cellar Hill, Teynham, where he handed me my money and insisted that I count it to make sure I had the right amount. This puzzled me but I did as he asked. I had to count it three times before telling him I thought he'd paid me too much. 'No I haven't, it's what I suspected; Ted has been taking five shillings per hundred poles for himself. It's now up to you to get your money back; I will tell you how much he owes you. It worked out to £1.5s.0d per week, making a total of £10. To say I was angry was putting it mildly. I was very hurt and disappointed to think he was willing to take money from Anne, the children and myself.

Before going home I went to my see my mother-in-law, Win, and told her I wanted to see Ted as soon as he got home. I knew he went to the pub before, and it made me angrier to think I was paying for his drinking. I hated to see money going in drink, and his wife short of money too. I heard enough about my very own father doing exactly the same thing; I find that so unfair and cruel.

I told Anne when I got home and that I had left a message with her Mum saying that I wanted to see him straight away when he returned from the pub. I was rather surprised when Anne said 'I'm not t stopping here when Dad comes, as he was a boxer during his army days and he'll start a fight'. I was quite prepared for that. I could stand up for myself, and it was for my wife and children. The bugger was going to pay me back. So when he arrived, Anne disappeared with the children, and he came in full of life after a few drinks.

I pulled the money out of my pocket and told him to count it. Why he said? Just count it I said. '£6.5s.0d, yes that's right', he said. 'How is it', I said, 'that you have been drawing that amount each week and yet you have only been paying me £5? What have you done with the rest of it?' His reply was something I could not believe.

'Well, I got you the job so I think I deserve it'. By God that made me mad. To think he would take money from his own daughter, children and son-in-law. He could see that I meant it when I told him he had to pay it back at £2.5s.0d per week over the next two months, even if he had to go without his beer. I'll give him credit – he did pay me back, and from then on we got on fairly well.

It was also then when Anne came to the rescue during the evenings. She went out to work at the fruit-packing station in Faversham. She had to cycle twelve miles there and back, or catch the bus, and I would look after the children. When the fruit packing finished she then started repairing silk stockings. These were unobtainable for several years after the war and she would earn about 6d per stocking (21/2p). It took her an hour to complete just one (bless her heart). There was very little money for anything other than living expenses, and life was getting difficult. It wasn't long before arguments started between us and I was getting frustrated. My whole aim was always to try and make a good life for Anne and the children. Pubs and drinking never did give me any pleasure, and work was the only thing ever on my mind. We were only living on £4 per week, and sometimes less. Without Anne's efforts we could not have survived, and I now only wish I had been more appreciative of her efforts.

My first lettuce crop was cut and radishes pulled mid April 1949. I sent some to London market and some I sold to the local vegetable shops. I had 95 percent success and the financial side was good. Tomatoes, runner beans, cucumbers and strawberries could only be sold to local individuals because of the high prices, they were fetching £1.10s.0d (or thirty bob) fora small punnett! On Sundays, I would take my bicycle loaded with them to a lay-by just above Norton Garage and sell my produce. It was nice little earner, with a lot of the local passing trade.

Going back to the time when Mr Chase held the first demonstration at my market garden, which was known as the cloche Nursery, I met a person who, with his wife, became a very good long time friend. His name was Cuthbert Osborne Dan (Danny) and they lived at Wingate Hill, Upper Harbledown near Canterbury in Kent in a very badly deteriorated wooden bungalow. This was such a shame as he came from a well-known Faversham family; with his father owned a wine merchant business and a large property known as the White House on Brogdale Road, Faversham. Danny had had a private education before the war. He was about twelve years older than me and was employed as a senior bank clerk before the war broke out. His wife was a little older. Apparently he got fed up seeing all the young lads going into the forces, and when he was thirty-three years old he volunteered, without the knowledge of his wife, for the Air Force. She wasn't very pleased, to say the least. He served until the end of the war but never went overseas and returned to the bank. (The bank had paid him all the time whilst he was away).

Not long after, his father died and the wine business was sold to provide for Danny's mother. Danny told me he was getting very dispirited with his job. Men below him before the war had got promoted above him, and he was not even being considered. After knowing him for a while I could understand why. He was such a lovely generous man; he would have probably given all the bank's money away.

Three years later his mother died, and as he was the only child he received a considerable sum. This gave him the chance he was looking for; he could now move on. He brought a small apple farm, Staines Farm, Upper Harbledown. Sadly, he had little knowledge of fruit growing and the place was in what was known as a frost pocket, so any late frost damaged the crop. Also, because of his generous attitude, salesmen found him an easy target.

He found himself buying a large quantity of fruit spray, apple boxes with his name printed on them (not necessary when he found out he could have got them for nothing from the Market), a new spraying machine, new ladders, etc. He was such a lovely man he could not say no to anyone. It was a very great pity and a sad day when he had to sell everything, including his Bentley, to move in to this badly run-down house. He ended up working for a dairy hygiene company. His wife Nina died first, and it was not long after that Danny died. I miss him very much.

Returning to Cloche Nursery, my market garden, we are now into 1949/50. I built a greenhouse, adding a boiler and hot water pipes, which enabled me to grown my tomato plants and cucumbers in trays and pots. This gave me a much larger number of plants under the cloches, which in turn produce fruit much earlier, and get a better price at the market. Everything was going well and we were making money. In November 1951, Annette was born and we were still in the prefab bungalow. We also knew we would have to move sometime soon to a larger house.

Running down beside the Co-op supermarket in Teynham High Street was a path, which ran all the way to the lower road connecting to the station line known as the Ash Path. On the left hand side near Teynham High Street end was the piece of ground that I had bought from Mrs. Akins, Cloche Nurseries, and on the right was another piece of ground, again belonging to Mrs. Akins. She would not sell this to me as the council had earmarked that for housing. Eventually these houses were built and we put our names down for one. However, it was another two years before ours would be ready. No. 8 Cherry Gardens was ready for us to move into. It was situated on the corner of Station Road and Frognal Gardens, Teynham.

It was a large semi-detached brick council house with three bedrooms and bathroom upstairs and a lounge, dining room and kitchen downstairs. We moved in when Annette was still a baby, and stayed there until 1963. Christopher, our last child, was born in March 1959.

The house was at the end of a row on a corner, so we had a garden that surrounded the house on three sides. In those days, gardens were large and the rooms inside were square and large. Although the boys had to sleep in one room, we were very comfortable there.

Life took on a hard-working pattern until sometime in the mid 1950s, when things started to get tough financially. Money was getting increasingly difficult to make from the market garden. Holland was getting over the war, and was moving fast back into their traditional market gardening, producing tomatoes, cucumbers, radishes and lettuces which were coming into our markets at least two weeks before mine, therefore reducing the return I was getting.

Sadly, I started to get into debt and that was something I had never been used to. I was getting very depressed, which in turn made life difficult for everyone around me, which encouraged a tension between Anne and I. It was at this time that Anne's mother, Win, encouraged her to join The Royal British Legion; in a short time Anne became the standard bearer for the Legion, which meant she was out more often. It was good for Anne to have another interest, but both difficult and easier, for us in our strained relationship. I was getting more morose and depressed, totally unaware that this was the start of a duodenal ulcer, hence the symptoms.

It was also at this time that I realized I would have to find a new way of earning more money and next door to the Co-op was a lean-to building being used as a watch repair shop. The person renting it was giving it up, unable to make it pay.

After speaking to a Mrs Oyler, the lady who owned the shop, and after discussing my idea with Anne, I opened a vegetable shop to hopefully earn the extra cash needed. Anne was running the shop for us, as well as looking after the children whilst I was working on the market garden. Unfortunately the returns on the shop were not enough, but at this time I met a gentleman called Barry Boucher. He had two large greenhouses at the bottom of Stockers Hill, Rodmersham, growing produce as I was. His greenhouses were heated as mine were, but one of my greenhouses had a broken heating pipe and Barry had some spares ones I could buy. Unfortunately, I was not in a position to pay him but he agreed to trade one of my irrigation pipes for his heating pipes, so we struck a deal.

We got into discussion about how I was having problems with the Dutch produce flooding the market, creating a glut of vegetables and which were pushing Barry's tomato prices down. He then came up with something that intrigued me. Apparently he had been asked on numerous occasions if he had a rotavator, and if he could he rotavate people's gardens. This was the time when there was a boom in house building, so there were many people with gardens needing mechanical help like the rotavator to sort out the ground. Of course I had one, and it wasn't long before I put an advert in the local paper and shop windows.

My only means of transport was by cycle and I couldn't drive; it was something I regret not learning whilst in the army, and as sergeant I was expected to but never did. I was never given the opportunity, and with hindsight I should have insisted. The only thing I did do was to learn to ride a motorcycle. This was done so that I could take over the sergeant major's job controlling traffic when we were on the road.

When the orders came in for rotavating I had no means of getting the machine to the job. However, a friend came to my aid. Bill Sillcock lived in Teynham, and he offered me the use of his car and trailer on the understanding tha he could borrow the rotavator to do his allotment. This arrangement worked out well for a while, but I knew that as more work came in that I would have to buy my own vehicle.

You have to remember I was running a market garden as well as keeping the shop stocked with produce and then I was about to take on another job of rotavating.

I am sure you have heard the expression that it never rains unless it pours… Well, that's what happened to me. Anne fell pregnant with Christopher, which eventually meant we would have to give up the shop and gradually the market garden. By selling the cloches, greenhouses etc it helped the money situation. I think I had somewhere near to £1000, which was a lot of money in those days, but I had to make sure I looked after it for living expenses.

Once the market garden had gone, I could expand on my gardening jobs, and I offered my services mowing peoples lawns, maintaining gardens and rotavating. I was lucky, in so far as I picked up several jobs, which helped. One was for Mr. Swann, a builder living in Teynham, who I got to know very well.

I was working hard and making reasonable money, more money than I had seen before. It was between £12.0s0d and £15.0s.0d per week, so I managed to give Anne some extra money and save some.

It was February 1957, when the news came from my sister Dolly, that my mother was ill at home. I immediately went to see her in Didcot, where they had moved to, after their house at North Moreton had been condemned. When I got there, she was trying to walk around; apparently she had fallen down and her back was causing her a lot of pain. She was 77 years old, which today it not a great age, but at the time it certainly was. The doctor had diagnosed a slipped disc, and told her she would have to lie flat on her back, on hard boards, for the symptoms to improve. Sadly, she refused, saying she was not going to be an invalid, besides which, she had to look after my Dad.

My sister Dolly use to visit them every weekend, but she lived a long way from mum, and she was working during the week. It was then that my sister Rose, who lived in Chiseldon on her own, decided to make her home with mum and dad. At this same time, I decided to learn to drive, and by the end of March I had passed my driving test and bought my first car. It was an old Morris, which I'd bought for £50.00, from a garage in Teynham called Ferrell and Bakers. The Morris had cable brakes, which were not very good, to say the least, nor was the car all that reliable, but it was my first car!

Full of pride, Anne and I would drive to the Radcliffe Hospital, in Oxford, to see mum. By now she had been admitted and we would try to visit every other weekend, knowing she was very poorly. Sadly, she died on September 14th 1957 and the following year Dad died, aged 89.

To make matters worse, Mr Ching fell very ill with cancer of the throat. and sadly died shortly afterwards. He was a very heavy smoker, sometimes smoking over 40 a day, which actually put me off. It was very upsetting to lose a third person who I was close to and respected.

Sadly, the ground of Cloche Nurseries started to overgrow, but I did not physically have the time to do anything about it at this time.

Then six months after Mr Ching dying, I received a letter from his solicitor, Messrs. Lett and Co, acting on behalf of the Ching Estate. It was asking me to repay the money I had received.

At the time when Mr Ching offered to help me, he also instructed a solicitor called Mr Arizona, from Sittingbourne, to provide me with any help I might need in the future. His words to Arizona and myself were that 'should anything happen to him I was to be treated as leniently as he himself would have done'. I was told, at a later date, by Arizona, that he meant that 'if I got into financial difficulties, I was not be chased for the money,' and that it would be 'written off as a debt to his company, but of course the ground would be handed over to the Estate'. All of this was explained to Messer's Lett and Co by Arizona. For the next two years, letters went back and forth between the solicitors, and with the advice from Arizona, I refused to let them have the ground. It was believed that I would be able to get building permission on the land.

The time now came that I had to get a vehicle of my own, and luck came my way. Our milkman, Jack Ramsden, was getting rid of his Volkswagen pickup and it seemed to me that this vehicle could be ideal. Only a week later, I received a phone call from a Mr. Churchly, who owned the garage on the A2 Norton Crossroads in Teynham. He had taken in the pickup as a part exchange on a new Volkswagen for Mr. Ramsden, and asked me to come and see him. He offered me the vehicle for £300.0s.0d on finance. Unfortunately, I could not afford the deposit of 25 percent, but again I was lucky, and a compromise was found. This was the first time I had any knowledge of hire purchase, but I knew I had to repay a certain figure each month.

I had now got the bit between my teeth and believed that I could make some real money. It was not long afterwards that I got a rotavating job that my old rotavator was unable to cope with; the ground was far too hard. Whilst travelling through Sittingbourne, I had noticed an agricultural machinery shop belonging to a Mr. Hales. It was next to Webb's, the hardware shop, in East Street, which is still going today, with Swale Borough Council Offices being on the other side.

In the window was a large, heavy duty, Clifford Rotavator, I knew it was the right machine for the work I was doing, and I often stopped to look at it. Mr. Hales saw me looking at it, and this particular time, he came out to ask if I'd like them to demonstrate the machine. Ah, that was just what I was looking for so of course I said 'yes'. I asked him to take it to the job where my old machine could not master the ground ,and within an hour the garden was completely rotavated ,making me £1.5s.0d.

The crunch came when Mr. Hales said he wanted a deposit of £50.0s.0d. Sadly, I told him I was unable to find that sort of money (in fact, I could have, but I did not want to ransack my savings, as I needed it for my next vehicle payment). He was upset, saying the machine was now secondhand due to the fact it has been used. This was just the thing I had secretly hoped he would say. So I offered him my old rotavator as part exchange, which he reluctantly accepted, but he was not a happy man. I had started to use my brains to get on! Mr Hales, however, made more money out of me in the long term as I purchased many other machines from him during the coming years.

Winter was drawing near, and with it, very little work coming in, but I had managed to save some money to offset this dip in work. I kept this quiet from Anne, as I needed the money for the van and machinery, and I was confident that over a period of time I would be able to make a better standard of living for all of us. I am not particularly proud of that now.

It was about this time that the executors of Mr Chings' estate started putting pressure on me to accept, and put in writing, the fact that I had received the money from Mr. Ching. I spoke to Arizona, and he advised me not to do anything as he would contact them pointing out Mr Chings wishes.

I was now reaching the lowest ebb in my health (duodenal ulcer), and at the same time I went to work in the paper mill in Milton, Sittingbourne. It was shift work, with shifts from 6am-2pm (mornings), 2pm-10pm (afternoons) and 10pm-6am (nights). The money I was getting was three times the amount I had been getting in1946. Anne was getting more money, which she needed, with four children to look after. Christopher was born in March 1959, Roger was now nearly thirteen years old, Royston eleven and a half and Annette seven and a half years old.

The shift work was taking its toll on my illness, and Anne was finding me increasingly harder to live with. I never once hit her ,as I saw how my father used to hit my poor mother, and I vowed never to reduce my conduct to that level. I used to shout and swear, though, which I now admit with absolute horror and shame. I did not realize until after my operation how duodenal ulcers could you drag your health down so badly.

It was now mid 1959, the children were getting older, and as everybody else had a television on the estate, of course they kept asking me for one. To keep the peace, I hired one from Radio Rentals in Sittingbourne. I could not afford to pay for one out right without leaving myself short of savings, which I was not prepared to do. I had been so short of money in the past that I was so reluctant to spend my hard earned savings. It was delivered on Saturday evening to the delight of the children and we all sat down to watch black and white TV.

At this time,the executives of the Ching Estate gave me an ultimatum: to either let them have the ground or they would make me bankrupt. It was not long after this distressing news that I met a gentleman called Mr Victor Franklin, an estate agent from Sittingbourne. He had contacted me to ask if I had a machine to be able to mow his paddock. The contract was worth £15.0s.0d a month so I went off to buy a new heavy duty mower; another hire purchase to add to list of HP agreements, bringing my total to £2000.0s.0d.

I was still working at the paper mill, but I would also load up my vehicle with equipment and go at 7am to do the gardening work, either rotavating, grass cutting etc. I'd take a sandwich and flask with me, and then,at 2pm, I would go back to the paper mill for the shift until 10pm. I continued with this routine for the next four years, sadly, and now my duodenal ulcer was getting worse which I was taking out on the children.

Roger left school in 1960 and used to come out and work for me. He was a really hard worker but unfortunately I did not really appreciate it at the time and would work him very hard. One day, to my utter shame, I put him on a job by himself, digging a garden by hand, as we could not get the machine to the rear garden. It was not until 6pm that day that I returned and found him still trying to get it done to make me happy! When I did not respond, the owner came out and gave me a real telling off (and rightly so) for not praising him. He also said, 'I am going to give him £5.0s0d out of your money, which he deserves, not the pittance (£2.0s.0d) you pay him'. I taught Roger to drive on private roads and sometime later I came to somewhat regret it.

It was also about now that the solicitors letters started coming in more often. I knew that it would not be long before bankruptcy proceedings would be taken out against me. The thought of bankruptcy did not worry me in that sense, but it did Anne, she was very upset and kept telling me to let them have the land.

I was as stubborn then as I am now, though, and I had other ideas. It was then that I approached Victor Franklin, the estate agent, telling him that I had a piece of ground in Teynham, on which I thought would get planning permission for building houses. We arranged to meet that night to view it, and he was positive that planning would be given. The access road would have to be constructed going from the new Frognal Gardens housing estate down to Frognal Lane though. This meant that a portion of the ground belonging to the Fox pub would have to be purchased. It transpired that Mr Franklin knew the estate agent of the Fox pub, which was fortuitous. Within two weeks, Mr Franklin had agreed to buy the land on behalf of Lion Construction Co. at Newington. The price was agreed, and was double the price I paid for it, but still not enough to pay all the costs involved.

However, I took the money and paid it into the bank, telling the manager to freeze the account and that I was being made bankrupt. If I had tried to use it I would have made more problems for myself, so my brain was working overtime. I was sure I would come out on the right side later on.

About one week after that, a court official called and gave me the bankruptcy papers. The following day, without any instruction, I went to the receiver's office in Rochester and met with the assistant, explaining why I was there. His reply was that I would have to wait until they had received the papers and they would inform me. However, we sat down and had a cup of tea, and he then explained how unusual it was for someone to come in so quick and voluntarily. I then explained every detail; going through everything carefully, and sharing that I had finally sold the ground, but had frozen the money in the bank.

I also explained I was trying to earn a living, doing garden work as well as working in the paper mill (my idea was to try and get his sympathy and it worked). The assistant said, 'wait a minute' and he went off to see the official receiver, a Mr Heath. I was called in to Mr Heath's office. He stood up and smiled, asked me to sit down and proceeded to ask how they could help. I was amazed.

'My assistant' he said, 'tells me that you seem to be an honest, hardworking, genuine person and I understand that you were in the war. It seems to me that you to have been treated very harshly. I have spoken to Mr Arizona, your solicitor, who I know very well, and he confirms all that you have said'. I understand that you are doing garden work as well as working in the paper mill at Kemsley.

I replied that I was hoping to turn the gardening work into a landscape company and then he started to ask me questions: 'Do youhave anything on hire purchase? Who are the Finance Companies?'

My reply was, 'Stanton's, United Dominion Co. and British Waggon Co.

'Right' he said, 'Are you married'? '

Yes I am', I said.

'Right' he said, 'I will phone these companies, right now, and ask them to transfer the HP agreements to your wife's name, will she agree?'

'Of course, she will agree,' I said, and within 15 minutes everything was in place. I had to promise him that I would not tell anybody what he had done. (I don't think it matters now after over 50 years).

Two weeks later, I was instructed to attend Rochester Court to answer the bankruptcy order. It took about one and half hours, and Mr Smith was the solicitor for the Ching Estate. He did his best to try and make me look like a fool. but the receiver stood up and asked Mr Smith, 'Do you realise that Mr Figg has sold the ground and placed the money in the bank to be frozen, so that you and other debtors will received a percentage of the money. He has not made any attempt to spend it, and I think you and your client should be very grateful for the honesty of Mr Figg.'

Mr. Smith had one more stab at me, asking what had happened about the landscape equipment that I owned and if it was being sold? The judge looked at me and the receiver saying, 'what about it'?

I replied, saying, 'I do not own any such equipment.'

Mr Smith pounced on that, saying 'I saw you in a vehicle with the words "Garden Cultivation" written along the side only yesterday and in fact on other occasions'.

'Yes' I said, 'but it belongs to my wife Mrs Anne Figg' which was confirmed by the receiver.

Well, poor Mr Smith had all the wind taken out of his sails, which was my only bit of pleasure.

The judge, Mr Phipps-French, started summing up the evidence saying 'from what I have heard, Mr Figg has been working all the hours he can to pay off his debts. It is a pity, Mr Smith, that your clients did not trust Mr Figg, who I am sure is doing his best to honour his debt. Unfortunately, I have to make Mr Figg bankrupt, but if he is prepared to come back to see me in six months time, I will consider his discharge.' The proceedings ended and within a year I got my discharge. In those days, it made headline news in the newspapers, but what really upset me was that they never thought to mention my discharge.

Landscaping work carried on during 1960 and I was still working in the paper mill but, sadly, I was getting more and more bad-tempered. Anne could not understand why I should be like this. She had gone to see Dr Birch and he suggested that I go in to see him. Anne finally gave me an ultimatum to either go and see Dr Birch or she would leave me.

I eventually went and he immediately diagnosed my symptoms as a probable duodenal ulcer and sent me for an X-ray. He was proved to be right, but it was not large enough to operate on and so he gave me tablets, which helped initially. Gradually, it started to worsen, but at least Anne knew what it was and what I was going through and she had been a nurse during the war.

Roger was still working for me and as I said earlier, I had taught him to drive. Of course, he was not old enough to drive on the road. I used to park the vehicle and machines on a piece of ground near the Ash Path and walk back to the house. One day, when I was out working, a friend came to me saying 'what was wrong with you last night? You drove straight past me when I was trying to get a lift home. I know you saw me and did not stop'.

I said 'I was not out last night, so it could not have been me or my vehicle, you have made a mistake.'

'No,' he said, 'the vehicle clearly said your name on it'. This started me thinking. I always left the keys in my coat, and I knew Anne would not take it without asking first, also I knew she was in the house at that time. So it had to be Roger.

It was a Sunday evening and Roger went out. I waited for a short while and then walked down to see if the van had gone. The van was not there! I went home, very cross, and told Anne. This being a Sunday evening during the summer, the roads were very busy with traffic travelling back from the coast. This was the time before the new M2 motorway was buil,t and all the traffic travelled through Teynham. Vehicles were nose-to-tail at peak times. Although I know Roger was a very good driver, he had no driving licence or insurance. In the end, I phoned the police, and told them to look out for him and bring him home at once. It was not long before they phoned me saying that they had found him and were bringing him home. Before he arrived, I had already decided that he should be prosecuted, although it was against Anne's wishes. The police thought this might stop him doing it again.

I took him to court in Faversham, where a Mr Dixon was sitting as the Judge. I knew him as he was the local farmer. The charge was read out and then Mr Dixon looked at Roger and asked how old he was.

'Fifteen Sir' he replied.

'Did your father give you permission to take the vehicle out?'

'No Sir' he replied. Mr Dixon carried on telling him the consequences of such an action. He told him how he could have killed somebody and that I would have had to pay all the costs. Mr Dixon then asked if his father was in court 'Yes, sir' I responded, and Mr

Dixon asked what I thought they should do with him. By then, I was feeling very sorry for Roger and questioning my own actions. I told Mr Dixon that perhaps I was to blame for teaching Roger to drive in the first place, and asked him to take this into consideration.

'Very well,' he said, but I don't believe that, as I too have taught all my children to drive at an early age.' He spoke to a couple of his colleagues, and announced that he would give Roger a warning. He told him that, should he appear again in his court, he would send him to a correction centre.

I thought this would be something that he'd never forget and that he would take heed. Unfortunately, he tested everything in life to the finest degree, and two weeks later he did exactly the same thing. I was furious and waited for him to come in. When he did I began hitting him. It's something that I will always regret, and it was the first time I had ever hit anybody, let alone my own son.

That was the end of Roger working for me and he got a job working in the brick fields in Conyer. It was unfortunately not long before he was in trouble again, but in a totally different way. The union that was in charge of the workmen were complaining that Roger was working too hard and at sixteen was showing the men up! At times, he was earning more than the men, because of piecework and he had been told to slow down or they would call a strike.

In the end, and thoroughly fed up, Roger decided to leave and join The Merchant Navy. He went to the Merchant Navy School in Gravesend and, as it transpired, I knew the captain there, a Captain Adlard.

Later, after Roger had been there for a while, Captain Adlard gave me all the work to do the landscaping at the new Merchant Navy School. It had just been built and he gave me all the details on how much I should charge. This was when I turned my garden cultivation business name to A.E. Figg and Son Landscapes. The work enabled me to buy a Massey Ferguson digger, which in time, my other son, Royston, learnt to drive. This was to be a great asset in as much as it enabled us to achieve much more work than by human hand alone. For example, we could dig a large number of tree-pits quickly, thus increasing their profitability, which helped to set me up for a long time.

Near the end of 1962, Lion Construction started building the bungalows on my old site of Cloche Nurseries. We were still living at Station Road in the council house. Anne was now using the old Morris and I would use the pick-up. Royston was nearly sixteen years old, Annette nearly eleven and Christopher nearly three.

Anne's interest in the Royal British Legion gained, and she was enjoying the freedom it gave her, as well as it being another interest apart from me and the children. She so enjoyed it.

I think that one of the things that stands out for me, during the time at Station Road, was when Christopher was three years old. I had decided to come home early one day to get a cup of tea before going on to another job. I parked the pick-up at the side of the house, on the corner of Station Road and Frognal Gardens. Unfortunately, I had left the keys in the ignition. The next thing I heard was a loud bang, and looking out of the window, I saw the vehicle across the road, crashed into some iron railings. Who the hell has done this? I asked to anybody listening. And, lo and behold, as I ran out to see, there was Christopher sitting in the driver's seat with a big grin on his face! I have no idea how he managed to open the door or climb onto the seat, as he was such a small child, but he obviously did. He also managed to turn the ignition key, which I had left in and I had not only left the brake on, but I'd also left it in gear! There is nothing much else I can say to that, totally my fault.

Fortunately, he had done more damage to the railings than to himself and the vehicle. I knew the tenant, a Mr Kirby, who by nature was a miserable man, and you can imagine how cross he was. I promised to pay for the repair but, rightly or wrongly, it just did not happen.

At this time, Royston was attending St Johns School in Sittingbourne, which was the same school that Roger attended. The difference between Roger and Royston was obvious; they were like chalk and cheese. They would both go to school looking extremely smart, white shirts all tucked into their shorts and polished shoes. When they came home, Roger's shirt would be hanging out, tie adrift, hair looking as though he had been pulled through a hedge backwards. Royston, on the other hand, would come home just like he had left the house;

immaculate. Apparently he was a very studious young man, and was well thought of by his peers and teachers.

Roger was a rebel, though, (he probably took after me) and remained as such for the whole of his short life. He lived life to the full, taking chances with his life that enabled him to achieve things that he wouldn't have, otherwise. Almost as though he knew that he would, he only remained on this earth until he was forty-three years old. Whereas Annette was quiet at school and studious, like Royston.

It was now the end of 1962, and the bungalows were nearly completed, with the exception of one plot. This was next to where I parked my vehicles, and it was then that I decided to ask Victor Franklin if Lion Construction would consider building me one on the plot at cost price.

I was beginning to make money at last, and was starting to use my brains and my gut feelings when making decisions. Work was coming in thick and fast and I was still working in the paper mill. I knew that, before too long, I would have to make up my mind as to whether I should make landscaping my main source of income. In the meantime, I started to employ part-time workers to help out; mainly men who were also shift workers at the mill. It gave them a few extra pounds and kept my customers happy.

Lion Construction contacted me with a message for me to go to their main offices in Newington and to meet with Mr Clark, the managing director. He gave me a plan of a three-bedroom bungalow saying 'will this be alright for you?'. It was difficult to take it in, our own place – again, my cheek had paid off!. The only problem was going to be how to pay for it. I decided not to tell Anne, keeping it as a surprise, but also just in case it went wrong. She knew I had the appointment with Lion Construction, and wanted to know about the meeting when I returned. I told her it was a landscape job they wanted me to do.

The time had to come when I had to decide what business route I should take. My mind was soon made up when I picked up a job which proved to be very profitable. I handed in my notice and finished the following weekend at the mill. Anne was worried and my in-laws disapproved, saying 'you tried before working for yourself and failed. You should think of your family first.' They obviously knew nothing of the bungalow, or the work I had in hand. They did not know the money I would be making. I was so full of confidence – I just knew I could do it!

It was now the end of March and the bungalow was nearly ready. Anne still did not know about it. I thought it would be a nice surprise, however it did not work out as I thought. Bert Mason, the foreman of Lion Construction, had already told my sister-in-law that 'this place' was for Mr Figg. She asked Anne when we were moving in and of course Anne knew nothing about it, but questioned me when I returned home that night. I told her that it was not true. About a week later, Mr Mason asked me what sort of colour tiles we wanted on the kitchen floor. I did not know, so the next day Mason went round to our house and asked Anne. She could not understand what Mason was talking about, saying to him 'why do I want new tiles on this kitchen floor, when they are still good?' It was then that Mason told her it was for our new bungalow. She was lost for words, and told him that he would have to wait until I got home to find out if it was true or not. She gave me a real mouthful for not telling her. I explained that I wanted it as a surprise for her, and that I had to find the money first. The price was half of the true figure of £1,200.0s.0d the real figure being £4,200.0s.0d – I wish we could buy something at that price now!

I was trying hard to find a way of raising money. I knew I could go to a Building Society, but I had to find 25 percent deposit, and I did not want to use the money I'd saved for the expansion of the landscaping business. This was when my friend Danny came to the rescue. He suggested I go to Swale Borough Council and ask if they would provide a loan. This I did and, lo and behold, they said yes! They asked how much I wanted and I told them that I wasn't sure, but asked them to value the bungalow first. This way it would help to decide how much I needed. Without telling them how much I was being charged for it, the council came back saying the value was £2,900.0s.0d. This meant there was a margin of £1,700.0s.0d. I told the council I would only need £1,400.0s.0d so I still had enough to pay the solicitor's fee.

We moved into the bungalow in April 1963, and all this came as a surprise to Anne's family, who thought I would never make a go of it after my bankruptcy. We were now paying another £16.0s.0d per month more than we were paying for rent on the council house.

Work came in thick and fast, and it was not long before I was employing full-time men. Not only were we doing gardens in private houses, but building contractors were asking me to do their work as well. This meant that I had to get another vehicle, as well as a Ford tractor with a front loader, a large rotavator and a 3-tonne tipper lorry. But, as you can imagine, the HP was going up, and it worried me for a while, but I had the value of the bungalow behind me, which was ok, all the time the money was coming in.

It wasn't long before I found out that contractors took several weeks before they paid, and then they kept a percentage back, so it was nearly a year before I got all my money. However, I was still getting private work and here the money was ready when the job was finished. It was cash so I could put it to one side.

Royston was at school, and he turned out to be one of the star pupils of St John's School. He must have been nearly eighteen years old when he left school and he came to work for me. He was now riding a motorcycle, but it wasn't long before he passed his driving test and was using the Bedford van that I had bought for the business.

I had a Welsh man called Taffy Edmunds, who worked for me at the time, and he could be a difficult man to say the least. Royston was new on the site, and Taffy took great delight in telling him what to do, and not in the best manner, which ended up with Royston walking off the job!

The result was that Taffy also left, so I was left to finish the job by myself. I can remember working until nearly midnight with a hurricane lamp. I needed that job to be done as quickly as possible, to enable me to get my money, and to start another job the following day. This gives you an idea of the amount of work I had on. It is hard sometimes to deal with staff because of different personalities and expectations.

Now, with just two people with me, I had to look around for others to take their place. It was a nightmare. I had customers chasing me to find out when I going to start their work and at the same time, I was trying to show the new men what I wanted them to do. I had to go around visiting sites and explaining to the customers why I was late starting their work. Fortunately, most of them understood my problems, and accepted my word that I would start as soon as possible. On top of this, I was suffering more and more from the duodenal ulcer, and I was getting more difficult to live with. I was bad-tempered, not eating very well and going to bed almost as soon as I got home. When I got up the next morning, I was a completely different person. The pressure of work was not helping either.

I remember one morning getting up and finding Royston was missing. He had apparently climbed out of the bedroom window early in the morning and hitchhiked to Monte Carlo in the south of France. However, on arriving, he had run out of money and had to go to the British Embassy and ask for help. They, in turn, contacted me asking for money to send him back . He eventually joined the Dover Dock Police.

Work was still coming in, and I was earning good money, but of course my expenses were going up almost every month, and I was on an overdraft from the bank. I did, however, have my private jobs so that helped.

I had been thinking very hard about buying a better car for Anne. I really loved her very much but I could not express it with words. I am not afraid to admit it, but there were times I used to cry with frustration when we argued.

I was on my way home, going through Bapchild, when I noticed a car in Pritchard's Garage which took my eye. It was a Sunbeam Rapier. I had seen this type of car before, and had always fancied it, but it was not the colour that I wanted. After a couple of days I could not resist it. It was very funny beacuse when I went into the showroom there was a woman who used to work with me at the paper mill. The look of shock on her face when I told her I had come to look at the Sunbeam Rapier was priceless.

'Albert' she said, 'you must be joking, have you been left money'?

'No', I said 'I have worked damned hard for what I've got.' And with that, I paid the deposit and signed the HP forms. I left my work vehicle at the garage and drove the car home.

I knew Anne was going to a Legion meeting that night. Outside the bungalow there was a lay-by where people would park their cars to go shopping in the village. Anne used to get very cross when the cars were parked right in front of our window, so this is where I parked it. I went indoors, not saying a word about the car (this was one of the ways of trying to tell her how much I loved her with a surprise). I remember her coming into the kitchen crossly saying,

'Somebody has parked their car in front of our window again, when I see them I am going to tell them not to do it again! How would they like having a car parked in front of their window?'

I had to smile when she said 'What are you laughing about, it's not funny. Anyway, I've got to go, your dinner is in the oven'. With that she picks up her coat, saying cheerio, see you later.

I followed her out, handing her the car keys, saying, 'Here you are, I think you had better have these.'

. 'What are these for' she said 'I've got my own'?

'No, that is yours out there!' I said. Well, the look on her face made my day! I then had to say: 'Now be careful, it is twice the size of your old one, and I would like to see you come back in one piece', as she drove off with a smile as big as the car., I could not have been happier.

The years went by, with work coming in, but I had to employ more men and buy another vehicle for myself, as all the others being used by the workman. Although I was helping out on jobs running behind, to try and hurry them up, I was also going around looking at other work that had to be priced for contractors and private jobs. These were the most important jobs if I wanted to save.

My ulcer was getting worse, and I was getting more depressed and difficult for Anne. Annette left school and went to secretarial college. Chris was nine years old and still at school. Royston was with the police in Dover Docks and Roger was in the Merchant Navy. He would often return home, on leave, when his ship was in the London Docks. He passed all the exams to become a chef, which amazed me as I could never think of Roger as cooking.

On his 21st birthday, on 1st June 1967, he was at home. I remember laughing when he told his mother he would do all the cooking, and that she should keep out of the kitchen and leave him alone. When he had finished, I have to admit everything was perfect, far better than most restaurant food, and the birthday cake was unbelievable. Roger left the Merchant Navy in 1970, and started to work as a chef in the restaurant for Cheeseman Stores in Maidstone, where he met his future wife Lorraine.

I eventually had to go into hospital to have the operation to remove my ulcer. Roger left Cheesemans and came to run the business whilst I was away. I have to admit, he made a good job of it. I was off sick for about three weeks, but he carried on working for me for another two to three years. I had to go into hospital twice more during that time, and there is no doubt he saved the business for me. For all his faults, and there were a number of them, including wrecking a Mini pickup which I had bought for him to use so he could see Lorraine, his girlfriend, who lived a few miles away in Sutton Valence, I have to credit him for that.

Roger married Lorraine in September 1970, and Daniel was born the following year, my first grandson. Royston had met Pat and they were married in the following June. Then Annette and Vernon married in September 1971. So three of my children were married within the space of one year, which just left Christopher at home.

It was also at this time that I heard of a company which was looking for contractors to install swimming pools. It was a case of digging the holes to a certain shape, erecting steel panels for the walls and placing the liner inside etc. Roger was very keen to have a go at this, so I made the arrangements to go to learn how to do it. We had our own digger, a Massey Ferguson, which was ideal for the digging out of the holes. The profit margin was good at almost 150 percent, which Roger and I shared between us.

It was not long, before Roger wanted to do the pool installing full-time, and go it alone. He was married now, and had a child, so he needed a larger income. He started his own business as an agent with the same pool company, Buster Crabb USA, who had an office near Kew Bridge.

I was still doing pools, but on a reduced scale, as I would only do the jobs where I could get my large digger on site. I was approached by another company, who made the side panels of fibre glass for the pools, instead of metal. The metal was prone to corrode within three years. I took up their offer, providing they gave me one to put in my own place at 32 Frognal Gardens, Teynham. We became the talk of the village – Christopher had so many friends once word got round – and during the summer months it was always in use. Christopher left school in 1975.

We were now in a position to be able to go on holidays, mostly in the West Country, to Cornwell, Devon and Dorset. We also went Somerset, where two of my brothers lived, Jack (Michael Henry) and George. Eventually, I was able to buy a caravan and travel abroad to the South of France, Switzerland, Holland, Germany, Italy and Austria. The best part of this was that Anne really enjoyed it whilst we were away from home, and we had wonderful holidays together.

One day early in February 1971, when I had come home for lunch, which didn't happen very often as I either took sandwiches or called into a café, two men came to see me. They owned a piece of land behind the Swan Pub which had greenhouses growing tomatoes, etc. In fact, they bought my greenhouses, so I knew them. I knew that I was getting short of room for all the machinery I had, and this was also the time that Royston decided to come back to work for me after having experience with other jobs.

They had come to see if I had any machines that could mow their spare land as they were going to sell it. The entrance to it was just up Lynsted Lane. I had great difficulties not showing my excitement, thinking this would be the ideal site for all my machinery. I asked how much they wanted for it, but it appeared that they already had a buyer, so I told them to come and see me if they changed their minds. I told them how much it would cost for me to tidy the site up, and obviously, I exaggerated the price, who wouldn't? I added that if they sold the land to me that they wouldn't need to pay me for the tidying up because I would have to do it anyway. Away, off they went, and within five minutes there was another knock on the door. There they were, standing in front of me again, saying that they had thought about it and decided to offer it to me, providing it could be settled within three weeks at the price of £15,000. I accepted straight away and told them to come back and see me that evening and that I would have a deposit ready for them. I didn't tell them how much, though, or whether it would be a cheque or cash. It worked well for me to keep a certain amount of cash available because I knew if I waved the sight of actual notes under their noses, they would be eager to make a deal. They had already told me that one of their daughters was getting married in a month's time and so they would need the money. Later in the day, my brain started working overtime, thinking how I could raise money without going back to the bank. I already had an overdraft and I did not want to pay more interest.

It was then that I came up with the idea. I hoped that if I put £5000 cash on the table they would want to put their hands on it quickly, never having seen so much within their grasp. I then took a chance, by writing out a letter showing the deposit paid and the balance due of £10,000 to be paid. At the bottom it stated that they would accept this over a period of two years – £5000 in February 1975, and the balance of £5000 in February 1976. They took the money and signed the paper hurriedly. Unfortunately for them, when they came to collect the balance, I had to point out the details on the document they had signed. It had been legalized by a solicitor, so an agreement had been entered into.

They were furious, so I said 'okay, you return the deposit of £5000 cash and I will draw up a new agreement and pay 10 percent of the asking price of £15000. You can pay tax on the £15000. However, if you agree to the original agreement, then the Inland Revenue will only charge tax on the £10,000 and we won't make any mention of the cash deposit given.' Of course they had already spent the cash, which meant they had no real alternative but to accept.

It was now mid March 1974 and the Swale Borough Council had a new engineer surveyor, who I got to know quite well, as I was doing a lot of work for him for the council. I found out that the land that I was already using alongside the bungalow in Frognal Gardens, for parking and storing the equipment, had been earmarked by the council to make way for a road towards Lower Road in Teynham. I spoke to the engineer about planning permission to use the piece of ground in Lynsted Lane I was purchasing as a Landscape Yard. His words were 'Don't bother Albert, just move in and say nothing to anyone and hope nobody mentions it.'

On numerous occasions, I had mentioned to Anne that I would like to find a piece of land and build my own place. Of course I would not do it with my own hands. On this piece of ground that I had bought in Lynsted Lane there was an old condemned house. An idea started to form – what if I had plans drawn up for a bungalow and apply for planning permission? I had already seen one which I thought Anne would like at a customer's house, who had just given me an order for a swimming pool. He gave me a copy of the plans and I got a local architect to copy them and then submit them to the council with a letter. It said that if permission was granted, we would demolish the old one, but if not, then I would rebuild it and build three garages. I knew they would be horrified at that. They felt that the access onto Lynsted Lane was not safe. I soon rectified this by getting rid of the old house garden, thereby doubling the width of the drive onto the lane. At the same time, I sold the top soil, never one to miss a business opportunity.

The plans were submitted three times, and each time they were turned down, saying it was not in the right position. I was so mad that I had another plan drawn up, putting the plan just two feet to the right, and with this in my pocket, I marched into Swale Borough Council offices and demanded to see the clerk to the council, a Mr Bassett. This gentleman had signed the refusal. I was told he was busy and he would not be able to see me. With that, I sat down and said I would wait until he did see me. I waited for three hours and in the end he came out. He was told that I intended to stop there until he saw me and if he did not I would give an interview to the local paper on his refusal. I gave him an ultimatum that I either got permission with this plan or I would start rebuilding the old house. The council's ruling, in those days, was that if there was a property on the site, you could demolish it down to the first floor (no further) and rebuild it, along with the garages. The council was unable to stop me, and before I left, he agreed that I could build a new bungalow on the basis of the plan I had given him. Before I accepted his word, though, I made him fetch another person to witness his approval. My dream had come true, and now I could build a place of my own and without a mortgage (I hoped). It had taken me two years, since 1974, to get what I wanted.

I had my own machinery to dig the footings, the bricks from the old house to use as footing bricks, water and electric on site, transport to pick up sand and cement and a sewage connection only at the end of the drive. In fact, the only service I had to pay for was the gas.

It was now early 1976, and the bungalow was on the way. The footings had been dug and concreted. I had already found a bricklayer, and with the bricks from the old house, it was not long before it was ready for the concrete oversight. This was laid during the weekend – my bricklayer had to go on another job for a week, and to make sure he came back it was necessary to keep 25 percent of his money.

It was at this time that we were doing a job for R.J. Barwick and Son from Dover. They were building warehouses along the Sturry Road, where today PC World/Currys have their store. These units were almost completed, and there was a large number of internal blocks left over which would be ideal for the bungalow, if I could get them at the right price. I approached Bobby Barwick and he sold them to me for £250 for 3000 blocks. This was less than half price, but I had to take them away over the weekend. I had to work like a navvy to get it done. I ordered the bricks, with a good discount, and picked up the sand and cement from Brett's quarry, so by the end of the weekend I was all ready for the bricklayer the following week. The secret of getting the work completed as quickly as possible is to make sure you have everything on site, so the bricklayer cannot say he is waiting for material and then walk off site, in which case I may have had to wait several weeks before he would return.

In June 1976 we moved in, without any mortgage. That made me feel good, and I had achieved my dream. The bungalow consisted of a large fitted kitchen, a large wide hall which serviced three bedrooms, a large bathroom and a large lounge with a dining room on another level. The lounge had patio doors that took up the whole of one wall which overlooked the garden. I had managed to landscape it into a beautiful lawn, wonderful flower beds and, in time, a frame over a seating area for vines to grow up, with a separate summerhouse. I was very proud and Anne was delighted with her new home. I had divided the land up into two halves, the top half was Royston's with its own entrance and the bottom half was ours.

It was around 1975 when we were informed of the devastating news that Christopher had kidney failure. He was 17 years of age, and although they could treat it with drugs to start with ultimately he would need to go on dialysis. When he was 21 years old, four years later, this came to pass. I managed to build another room on the end of the bungalow which looked out on the garden for a dialysis room, which the hospital paid for and stocked with all the necessary equipment.

After Christopher was trained by the medical staff in the use of the dialysis equipment, he managed to put himself onto the machines, often with the help of Anne. Anne had been a nurse in the war so her training became very important. One of the most terrible things I can remember was when he would suddenly and often become engulfed from head to foot with cramp and would cry out in pain. Anne would have to massage him very quickly to get some feeling of normality back to his limbs. This was often due to the extent of how much blood and fluid was taken off and put back into his body. It was a huge responsibility for Christopher to ensure that all his levels (such as potassium and haemoglobin, to name only two) were in the right safety area.

He continued throughout the rest of his life on dialysis. After eleven years, he had his first kidney transplant. This lasted about six years, which meant he went back onto dialysis for another three to four years before another transplant. This did not last as long, and he was eventually back on dialysis. This would ultimately take its toll on his body, but in all those years of medical intervention he never complained, and tried to carry on with his life in as normal a way as was possible. He was always smiling, with a cheerful happy-go-lucky attitude.

Work was still coming in, and Anne and I were now frequently having holidays all over Europe for which I had bought the caravan for.

We both had our own cars, and it wasn't long before we were travelling by plane to places I had only previously dreamt about. Madeira, Majorca… Royston was doing the same, but mostly to Florida.

It was around this time that Roger started to get severe trouble with his back, which made it increasingly difficult for him to carry on with his work building swimming pools. He eventually had to give it up and go into hospital for an operation on his spine. After that, he was unable to bend down continuously so had to give up constructing swimming pools. He decided he would like to go back into catering, but this time operating a mobile van whereby he could go around shows and sports arenas and such. I bought one for him, and it proved very successful. It was not long before he expanded the business by delivering sandwiches to office staff with the help of his wife Lorraine and another vehicle. It was sometime later that Roger's marriage started to go wrong. They talked it over and decided to try and make a fresh start by emigrating to Australia. They sold everything to raise the money, and off they went. It wasn't long before Lorraine decided she didn't like it there, and she returned to the UK with the children, whilst Roger was out working. He knew nothing about it, and returned to the UK soon after as he was missing the children.

He came to help me as a foreman, with a view to taking over the business when I retired. Again Lorraine and Roger talked, and it was agreed they would return to Australia on the proviso that Roger went first, securing a house and a job, after which she would follow with the children. Very sadly, this was not the case; Lorraine was having an affair.

Roger returned, devastated, and threw himself back into mobile catering. He bought a vehicle on HP with a deposit from me.

In 1980, Royston was still working for me. It was now getting nearer to our ruby wedding anniversary in October 1982, and I was saving for something very special. For years I had been saying I would like to travel around the world, not knowing if I could afford it, and not knowing where to start and where to finish, so I saved. It was then that Annette brought me a globe. Whilst looking at it one night, Anne remarked she would like to go to Tonga to see where Queen Charlotte lived. She was so much admired by people in England when she came for our Queen Elizabeth's coronation, and for refusing to be covered when it rained and the big smile on her face when waving to the crowds.

So Tonga became my prime target, and I wanted to be there for new year's eve, so I started to map a route. I kept everything to myself, not telling Anne anything of what I was planning. 'Where are we tonight?', she used to ask me, when I was looking at the map; my reply was always the same – somewhere in the Pacific. Eventually, I came up with a planned route.

First would be Hamilton, the capital of Bermuda, and then on to Las Vegas via Phoenix, Los Angeles, Hollywood; then Hawaii and Pearl Harbour, to see where the American fleet was sunk by the Japanese, which had brought the Americans into WW2. From there, we flew to Suva, the capital of Fiji. Whilst there, we met a New Zealand couple who had been seconded to work for the Tongan government in order to help construct their electricity infrastructure. We mentioned that our next destination was Tonga, and they then suggested that we go with them the next day, new year's day. They told us that they would get us the best hotel in Apia, the capital of Tonga. I had already told them Anne wanted to meet the Queen of Tonga and that was the reason we were going there. We got to the hotel, and we were treated like royalty. This was New Year's Eve, 1981; we had crossed the time zone and we were now one day behind. What happened next was like something out of a Cinderella pantomine. I invited the couple to dinner that night as a way of saying thank you. While we were eating, the manager came up to me to say that I was wanted in the office. I thought 'My God, what I have done wrong?'

When I walked into the office, there a man dressed in a white suit with gold braid and a cap to go with it. I have been instructed to invite you and your wife to the New Year buffet at the palace', he said, 'and we must be there before midnight'. I couldn't believe my ears. I remember saying 'You're joking!', 'No, sir', he said, and he read out the invitation again. I remember walking back to our table in a daze, wondering how it was possible that the King and Queen of Tonga knew we were there. Anne was concerned when I got back, asking me what had happened. I told her about the conversation, and that we had an invitation to the palace for New Year's Eve buffet, and that we had to be there before midnight. It was only then thatI noticed our friends were smiling; they had arranged this for us. It was now nearly eleven o'clock. Anne was so excited that she could not finish her meal; she kept saying 'I must go and get dressed! A good job I brought an evening dress with me!' She shot off, telling me not to forget to phone a taxi. After she had gone our friends told me that the palace was only just up the road and that we could easily walk there. I didn;t want to spoil her night, so we got a taxi.

It took us literally five minutes to get to the palace. The taxi stopped by the side of a dirt track, where two soldiers were leaning against the wall, smoking. They took very little notice of us, only pointing up the track to what looked like a white timber house; nothing like the castle we were expecting. There were fields on all sides and, and there were chickens and pigs running around at the front of the house. As we arrived, we found a lot of people waiting.

The house was much bigger than we first thought, with a large veranda. At midnight, we were accompanied by the sirens of a police escort, the King and Queen arrived. Apparently, the King always read the New Year's Eve service in the church.

The King was enormous, and he was wearing what looked like a sack around his waist. The Queen was, in complete contrast, quite petite. They both came up to us, and we had a brief chat as they were interested in the fact that we had come from England. After about twenty minutes, a member of the staff called out 'Would Mr and Mrs Figg please go first to the buffet'. We could help ourselves, and then everyone else would follow. I could see everybody looking at us, wondering who we were that we should lead the way. I shall never forget the look on Anne's face, it was beaming.

We spent the rest of the week there.

Our next stop was Western Samoa, at the well-known hotel called Aggie Grey. Aggie was still alive then, in1982. She was in her 80s and could still hula dance. The hotel was a famous spot for the navy during the pacific war in the 1940s. Aggie didn't mind how they spent their money, whether it was on booze or girls. It's also alleged that she had had an affair with the then King of Tonga.

All these islands in the Pacific are friends of New Zealand and Australia, who help them in numerous ways. For example, they provide roads and electric power lines; these islands would be very much worse off it was not for these two countries.

I knew whilst we were there that the Russians were trying to make headway into the Pacific by offering to build a new airport in Samoa and the King and their parliament were humouring them, knowing very well that the Americans would not allow it to happen, and that they would in time build it. The Pacific was and still is too important, especially during the Cold War between 1945 and the 1980s.

Fiji, Tonga and Samoa were no doubt one of the highlights of the four-month holiday. They are well-named the 'Friendly Islands', as everybody was always smiling, laughing and enjoying life. We were treated to them cooking for us in the ground, as they have done for hundreds of years. They would dig a hole, light a fire by rubbing sticks together and place stones on it until they were red hot. The food was absolutely brilliant.

For most of the time we travelled around in a tour bus, apart from hiring a car in Fiji. The bus we had in both Tonga and Samoa was very much the worse for wear; with very hard seats and no cushions, it looked as though it had just come out of Steptoe's yard. Everybody enjoyed every minute of it. One of our trips was to a sandy beach and we had to travel through a forest. It was just a dirt track, and it was absolutely hilarious. We were being tossed all over the place, but when we got to our destination it was stunning; pure white sand, and water that was so blue and clear that you could see to the bottom of the sea bed for at least a mile out. A few yards into the water were two large stones, but I was never very keen on going into the sea, as the waves made me feel giddy; I did pluck up enough courage, however, to go and sit on these two stones. Anne did the same. The water was so salty and I thought I could have easily floated in this without having to try and swim. Sadly I did not have the nerve, but to see the small fish of all colours swimming around our feet was very enchanting. Then a picnic on the beach… What a wonderful, magical day. The Samoan Islands, as a matter of interest, is where Robert Louis Stevenson, the author of Treasure Island and many more, lived in his later life and subsequently died. I can see the peace he would have breathed in and absorbed to enable his writing to continue.

From there we flew to New Zealand, where my brother Tom had emigrated in 1963 to Auckland with his wife Flo. I did not tell him I was coming, and I asked the taxi driver if he could find me a hotel near to his address. The taxi driver went one better and said he could find me one which looked down onto Tom and Flo's house. After settling into the hotel, I phoned him.

'What's the weather like out there? It is snowing like hell here in England'

'Yes, I have seen it on the TV news' he answered. We chatted for a few more minutes, then he handed the phone to Flo, saying it's Albert to wish us Happy New Year. She spoke and when I answered she paused for a few seconds. 'Where are you'? Tom, hearing this, said 'He's in England'. 'Oh no he's not, he's here. When a call comes from England there's always a pause before there's an answer and there is no pause, so he must be here'. 'Okay, look out of your window', I said, and there was me standing waving. It wasn't long before they were both in the hotel. It was good to see them. It was also the last time, as he died four years later. At least we had a good time altogether in North Island.

From there we flew to Tasmania, Australia; Hobart being the capital. This was the place Roger decided that he would extend his stay whilst he'd docked there when in the Merchant Navy as a chef. He'd jumped ship and gone to work for a road construction company driving diggers and graders, until he was picked up by immigration and sent back to his boat. I was speaking to him one day and he'd mentioned that on our trip we must stop off in Tasmania and travel on the road he helped build. Tasmania received the convicts transported from England to Philips Prison. We managed to see the prison, which looked a very daunting place. It was here that most of the British people started life after their prison sentences, sometime I believe in the early 1800s. We were there in early 1982 and it was very hot; all the grass was brown and tinder dry. Fires were starting everywhere.

We flew from there to Melbourne, Australia. My sister Margaret lived in Canberra so we hired a car and drove to see her. Margaret was not one of the best people in my life, but I felt that I must keep the promise I made to my mother when she was dying that I would keep in touch with all the family. Rightly or wrongly, I like surprising people, so we never informed anyone that we were coming. We drove around the area where Margaret was living with her daughter Irene (who was always called Bunty, it was the only name I knew her by). I saw her in the garden with Bunty., We stopped and asked if they knew where Mrs Troughton lived. Margaret looked at me and said 'that's me'. Bunty looked up when I said 'Hello Bunty!' They were speechless, and then Bunty shouted 'It's Uncle Albert!, He's the only one that would call me by that name!'

We stopped at Margaret and Bunty's for two nights, and then drove to Sydney for another two nights before flying on to Cairns, well known for the Great Barrier Reef. We went out on a glass-bottomed boat to view the reef; what a wonderful and magnificent sight! It's something that should not be missed. We also spent two nights on Green Island. It's only about one mile square, with six chalets. Afterwards we went back to the mainland and took a coach tour through the rain forest and the peanut growing area, and then a train ride back to Cairns and back to Sydney.

We then hired a car and drove back to Canberra and Bunty's house. It was our intention to drive to Melbourne and fly onto Western Australia, Perth and Freemantle, where my sister Minnie was living. Another surprise – she didn't know we were coming. Then Margaret dropped a bombshell on us; she'd decided to come with us. It was the last thing I wanted. We did not get on together, and Minnie's children disliked her. Anyway, there wasn't much I could do about it, so we set off. I must admit that she was as good as gold during the trip, and paid her way. This was the end of January 1982 and apparently it was Minnie's birthday on the first of February; this was the reason she wanted to go.

We arrived in Perth airport and then drove to Freemantle where Minnie lived. On arriving in the centre I phoned Minnie and told her I was a friend of her brother Albert and he had asked him to make contact with her. I told her where I was, but unable to find out where she was living. I told her where I was parked. And she told me to stop where I was so they could come and find us. She nearly fainted when she saw who it was. I love the look on people's faces when meeting each other after so many years. We spent a week there, firstly having aa couple of nights in a motel; after that, Minnie's two sons Stanley and John moved out to allow us to spend more time with Min. Also, as I said, there was no love lost between them and Margaret.

It wasn't long before Margaret and I started to fall out. She thought she could still treat me like the little boy she knew in the 1920s. As it happened, it was Minnie's 70th birthday so we got together and organized a party. I did not have much cash on me and I had already told Stanley and John that I would draw some cash out the following day and pay them then. Of course, Margaret knew nothing of this arrangement, and started again accusing me of not paying my way. That did it. I asked her why she'd wanted to come here just to upset everyone. From then onward, we never spoke. That was the last time I ever saw her. She died, I believe, in 2005.

Our next destination was Mauritius in the Indian Ocean. Not avery wealthy place; there is no old age pension, and when the husband dies there is no income for the widow. In 1982, the main income came from sugar cane and tourists. We spent one week there, and then on to Nairobi to see the wildlife. Unfortunately, we had to stop at Mombasa due to a hijacked plane which had landed at Nairobi, with the hijackers demanding fuel to be allowed to fly on to England. We had to wait several hours in the steaming heat with nothing to eat and very little to drink. This had to be bottled water, which was in short supply. That's a place I never want to see again.

We eventually reached Nairobi and got settled into the hotel, having been warned to take only authorized taxis and tourist coaches for the safaris, and when out walking to always keep to the main streets. Our first safari was to the water hole where the Queen spent time during her honeymoon; it was whilst there she had been given the news of the death of her father King George VI. She arrived back in England as Queen Elizabeth II. The visit to the water hole is something I shall never forget of all the highlights of our four-month tour. We spent one night in what was known as Tree Tops, a hotel built on wooden stilts with a veranda overlooking the water hole. I spent almost all of the night watching the animals; I was just mesmerised. Anne had gone off to bed, and was woken up by the staff when the elephants came. Whilst I was sitting there on my own, out of the corner of my eye, I noticed an animal coming out of the tree and started walking along the plank of wood which acted as an armrest where you could also place your food and drink. Some of the people had left food on it and this lemur came up and helped himself. I sat perfectly still, and managed to get a photo of it as it made its way towards me. (Don't ask me where it is, as I have hundreds if not thousands of photographs). The following day we went on Safari in a coach, there was so many different animals I am unable to remember them all, some I do remember though like the lions, tigers, cheetah, zebras… I would recommend this trip to anyone.

Our next place was Israel. I am certainly not religious, but I was very impressed; the problem was the arrogant and forceful attitude of the Jews. The taxi drivers and the street traders being the worst JI'd like to give you one example, from when we were going on to Cyprus. I had called a taxi to the hotel to take us to the bus station. We had been told before leaving Nairobi that it was cheaper to go by bus and ignore the taxis, as they were charging tourists treble the bus price. It came to our attention when we arrived in Israel. We waited at the bus stop, but a taxi driver was very insistent that the last bus had gone. We ignored him and a bus came along. When we were leaving, the driver insisted he drove us to the airport. I kept telling him I wanted to go to the bus station, and we sat there arguing. In the end I had to shout and swear and this worked. I found out later that they don't expect this and don't know how to handle people who do this. With that I had no more trouble and he took us to the bus station.

We arrived in Cyprus in mid March, 1982. It was now four months since we had left home, and now we were in the place of my last posting during my army days. IWhilst in Israel we met an officer of the Royal West Kent Regiment, who was serving in Cyprus with the United Nations, helping to keep the peace between the Turks and the Greeks. The island had been split between the two countries after the Turks invaded the island. When we arrived he invited us to lunch in the officers' mess, and took us on a tour of the island. The first place I wanted to see was the prison where I was a staff sergeant and sergeant mess caterer; unfortunately, the road was closed to the public but I could see it in the distance. That brought back memories.

Once back home again in England I was wondering what problems with the business I was going to face, but everything seemed to have gone well with Royston in charge. Many of the men, however, were glad to see me back. Our Ruby wedding anniversary (forty years) was in October 1982, but we had travelled one year early. I had had the money, and I was afraid it might disappear beforehand. The children had got together and organised a wonderful surprise lunch with loads of friends including my brother Jack (Michael Henry), and my best man at our wedding Fred Keogh

When Royston came back to work for me, he was renting a house. He'd never been in the position to be able to buy his own. It happened that houses were being built on Station Road. Teynham, and to give him a start, I gave him the £1000 for the deposit on one of these houses.

Shortly after, I felt that I should help Christopher and Roger to buy their own houses too. A piece of land came on the market in Water Lane, Ospringe near Faversham. I bought it with planning permission for three houses, one for Roger and one for Chris. The third house was for Steven, the son of a friend of mine called Charles Lister. I would finance it, but they would have to help in the evenings and weekends; they readily agreed. It was up to me to buy the materials and build the houses. Chris had got married to Rosalyn and was living in a caravan in my yard. They eventually rented a house in Ospringe; this was around about 1984.

Royston had been having holidays in Florida, and on one of his returns he told me that he had bought a piece of land out there and was going to build a house on it as an investment. It turned out that he and Pat had already made plans to live in Florida and were selling their house. Unfortunately, they went without saying goodbye to me or Anne. It was 1989 before we spoke to each other again. It's always a regret to fall out with ones children.

A few years later, Roger said he was getting fed up with living in England, so I suggested he went to Florida and find Royston. I thought Royston might put him up until he could get a job and a flat. Roger found him and he let him stay. He got a job the following day. Roger was never afraid of work and would have a go at anything. He gradually met other people and eventually secured a job on the Greyhound buses. It was whilst doing this that he met a lovely American girl called Pattie and they married in August, 1988. We went to their wedding in the States and took his two children. Whilst we were there, I took them all on a trip to see the Niagra Falls. It was an amazing experience for us all.

I was now back on my own again at the age of 64. I was expecting to retire at 65 and had hoped that Royston would take over the company. Now, this couldn't happen. I was in the habit of visiting my nephew John at weekends, the eldest son of my brother Jack. John was living in a large farm house next to the old Hersden coal mines; it's now an industrial site, just outside of Canterbury. Whilst there I met one of his sons, Paul, a school teacher in London. To be honest I was not very impressed with him; he was very arrogant, and I was discussing with John that I might have to take on a manager to help with the growing amount of work I had. Apparently Paul was listening very carefully to what I was saying to John and it was later that evening Paul phoned and asked if I would consider giving him the job as my manager. I couldn't think why he would want to give up a good job as a teacher with a pension at the end of it. I told him that he would have to come and spend a week with me first to see if we could get on together; this was agreed and he came the following week. Anne took an instant dislike to him, and couldn't believe I'd take him on, saying he was arrogant and full of his own importance. That week I took him around to different sites and to a meeting with a very important client.

On our way home he came up with some words that took me by surprise. 'I don't know how you can do without me'. That did it; I told him the job was his. Little did he know what I was planning. Albert's brain was working overtime… Anne was furious, and told me she would not work with him (she had been doing the accounts since Royston left in her spare time).

Anne found herself a job with Cardy Constuction Company. I was their landscape contractor, and her being in that job helped in a way, as I to got paid by them very quickly, which was useful. Paul came to work for me, and moving from London to Boughton, and I gave him a vehicle to use. It was now mid 1985, it didn't take me long to work out my next move. I let him have his own way for a week or two; his arrogant attitude was showing more and more, which was just what I wanted. I started to get touchy with him, using a few swear words at him and calling him a useless fool, telling him he would never make a good manager. That brought him down to earth with a bump, but I didn't get rid of him as I had other plans. I left him on his own again for a while. I knew my plan was going to work, and it wasn't long before he was back to his old ways, trying to tell me how to run the business. I gave him several important jobs, like pricing some work and buying trees and shrubs at the best prices; I checked all his work, which was annoying to him. On the way to another job, he started moaning about me not trusting him and that he knew what he was doing. That was just what I'd been waiting for. I stopped the car and went berserk with him. 'Why don't you buy me out, if you think you can make a better job than me?' He damn near snapped my hand off; bingo. I told him how much I wanted for the company, including the name, A E Figg & Son, Ltd. That was worth more than the landscape side. I set the figure very high on purpose. I knew he would have great difficulties raising the finances; he had no money of his own or any collateral. He went round and round the banks, but nobody was prepared to help. After a while, he had to come back to me saying he was unable to raise the money.

I wasn't surprised. I had another trick up my sleeve. I knew a nursery and garden centre near Ashford called Beuchamp Clarke, who were interested in buying me out. I sent Paul to them to buy trees and shrubs. I knew very well he would start talking about me selling up. It was a matter of days before he came running to me, saying he could raise the money. I had to smile… He wouldn't tell me where the money was coming from, but of course I knew. The only sticking point was that he thought I was asking too much, so I cut the price but put a proviso in the contract that he would pay me a weekly wage for two years as a consultant, which in the end made it up to the figure was asking for it in the first place. In April 1986, the contract was signed, which brought to an end my landscaping. Or so I thought.

I was now at a loose end. I had made a nice garden and that kept me busy for a while. I erected a lean-to greenhouse and started to grow my own bedding plants and finished up with a garden fit for any landscape gardener. As for the houses in Water Lane, Ospringe, Christopher moved into his but Roger and Steven Lister decided to sell theirs and take a profit. Then I felt I wanted to know more of the Figg side of the family. I knew my mother and father came from West Sussex, Childington near Pullbourgh. I knew my mother's maiden name was Streeter, so I drove down to Childington and started asking if any one new anyone of that name. I was directed to a council house on the other side of the road (apparently Streeter is a well known name in that area) and I knocked on the door. Before anyone answered, a elderly gentleman called out that there was nobody in, and that they had gone shopping. I asked if the people's name was Streeter and I told him what I was looking for and that my mother's name was Streeter. He came up to me saying that he knew me. I didn't think so as I'd never been here before, but he was sure he knew me. I never told him my name, but he asked me to come into his house for a cup of tea; apparently he had not long since lost his wife, and I felt sorry for him. He kept saying 'I'm sure I have met you before somewhere You're very much like a friend of mine'. Asking what his friend's name was, he answered 'George Figg.' I could not believe it. Here was I looking for my mother's relations, and now I have got the Figg Family as well. At this point, I told him that Figg was my name and he said I was a living image of his friend George. It was an exciting moment for me, and all I wanted to know is where this person lived. Apparently, he lived just down the road, and he gave me the address, which was only a five minute drive away.

I had a photo of my mother, with me. She was standing beside her brother Tom and his wife Nellie. In 1937, my sister Dolly had taken mother down to West Childington to see if she could find him – apparently she looked after him when her mother died at the age of thirty-eight. She died just after having her twelfth child, Rhoda. I found George Figg's house and he was in his garden digging. I stopped in my tracks, because as I was watching him, I could see my own father with his back towards me. Every move he made was just like my dad, it was uncanny. I knew right from the moment I saw him, he was a relation. I went up to him saying, 'I think you are a related to me, my name is Albert Figg,'

'I shouldn't think so', he replied, 'but come in and have a cup of tea and meet mother'. It is the British custom to offer tea to everyone that calls. We sat down and started talking and I stared telling him about how I was searching for my mother's relations, and it was only by chance that I found out about him from his friend. It was then that I brought out the photo of my mother and her brother and showed it to him. He had to look at it twice before saying 'that is my Uncle Tom and Aunty Nellie but I don't know the other woman'. I explained that she was my mother and Tom was her younger brother.

As time goes on, the story gets even better. It turned out that his grandmother was Charlotte Figg, my father's eldest sister, and that his father was Herbert Figg, Charlotte's son. Now I was puzzled, because how was it, that Charlotte's name was Figg and her child's was name Figg? It turned out that Charlotte had given birth to Herbert in February 1882 before she married the boy's father, Herbert Short, in October of the same year. So, he had to take his mother's name. Herbert Short was living with them as a lodger. It was a common thing in those days to have lodgers. The money came in handy to help keep the large families – ten children was normal, sometimes more.

George came out with even more names. Norman Streeter was my Uncle Tom's son. He could only tell me the village where he lived, so when I got home I found his phone number and contacted him. He would not believe me until I mentioned his father's name and his wife Tom and Nellie (Short). It turned out that Tom had married Auntie Charlotte's daughter. It was getting more and more interesting, so I arranged to meet him. When we met up, I showed him the photo of Uncle Tom and my mother and he had to agree that we were cousins. As we talked, he gave me more names and addresses of cousins in Sussex and Hampshire. He told me about two sisters, Gert and Daisy, who were living together and they were his aunties. He gave me their address and I went to visit to them both. They were well into their eighties and had all their faculties. They had heard of my mother, but had never met her, but they recognized Tom in the photo. Thank goodness for that photo otherwise I would not have found so many cousins. They gave me a piece of paper with lots of names on it including Auntie Charlotte's and others. Over the years, I have been trying to find out more about them with little luck, but I keep trying.

Whilst riding around, I found another five cousins. I then started to think that perhaps, at sometime, I should start a family tree. It was also now that I thought about moving house once again - the garden was getting too much for me to manage – the arthritis in my knees was getting more painful, and I knew, at some stage, I would not be able to walk, unless I had replacement joints. I talked it over with Anne. She was not to keen about moving – she loved this place, but I said to her, 'we don't want the place to go wild'. The time to move was now, as the house market was at its highest, particularly for bungalows. An estate agent valued it at £210,000, so we decided that we would buy another place, or find a piece of ground and build another. Lady Luck was on my side again. When I collected my paper from the shop, I met Trevor Crispen, the owner of the fish and chip shop in Teynham. We were talking and I mention that I was thinking of moving, and asked if he knew of any ground with planning permission? Right out of the blue, he told me he had a piece of land in Station Road, next to his house and the doctor's surgery. I have been very impulsive all my life. I would come up with a idea, think about it for while, and then jump in the deep end. I'm pleased to say it has work out, nine times out of ten. My motto has always been 'if you don't ask, you don't get anything; there are only two answers, yes and no'.

It was now 1987 and the bank readily lent me the money to buy the land, knowing very well I had plenty of collateral in the bungalow. I wanted to build another bungalow, but the ground was not wide enough, so it had to be a house. The design of the house really sorted itself out. Our son, Chris, was still on dialysis and divorced. So, I needed a bedroom on the ground floor with a shower room, a dialysis room, a lounge so Chris could have his friends over, and also veranda. Anne wanted a bedroom upstairs, next to the bathroom, and we also needed a spare bedroom for visitors. In addition, we needed a kitchen, a dining room and a lounge for ourselves. I originally intended to put the garage under Chris's bedroom, but this was ruled out by Chris and Anne, owing to the smell of petrol/exhaust fumes and the fact that we would wake up Chris when we came home late. I decided to put the garage at the top of the garden, which in the end proved to be the right decision. I could build the garage first and then I could put the material for building the house somewhere dry.

We started building in September 1987, and moved in June 1988. In August, we went away to Roger's wedding. I remember when we were waiting at the airport to see him off, Roger was missing. I noticed him walking away, and I had to run to catch him up. He was crying and he said he could not stand there knowing that he would not be seeing us or the children for quite a while. I also knew he was short of money, having spent too much on the wedding, so I slipped a hundred dollars in his pocket, and assured him that we would come out again next year. He seemed to pull himself together, started smiling, and waved goodbye. Little did I know that this would be the last time I would see him alive. In June 1989, Anne and I sat down to watch the Last of The Summer Wine, one of our favourite TV programmes, when the phone rang. Anne answered it, and then called me to the phone, saying it was a hospital in America. The voice at the other end just said our son had been killed and that we should contact the American Aviation Authorities. I made contact with them, and was informed that Roger's plane had crashed into the sea off Daytona Beach and that he had drowned. This was June, 1989.

I haven't yet told you about Roger's great love of flying. He learnt to fly whilst in Australia and when he came home, he bought an old Cessna plane. He repaired it to such a high standard, that when the British Civil Aviation Authority inspected and issued the certificate of air worthiness, they congratulated him on the quality of his work. He was a good pilot, but I would never fly with him; he used to put the wind up me when he flew over the bungalow very low and waggled his wings, but that was Roger the 'daredevil'. For most of his life, and whilst in America, he got a job flying and towing large advertising and announcement banners along the coast line of Daytona Beach. I saw him doing it several times, and to me it looked very dangerous. I prayed every time.

I had a premonition that something would happen to him one day, and now that day had arrived. We were devastated, and on top of that, we had to inform his children Daniel and Teresa and his wife Pattie. Unfortunately, she had to go to identify the body, and to make matters worse she was pregnant. It was Anne who suggested that I should speak to Royston, and suggest that he should go with Pattie as support. I had not been in contact with him since he left England, so I had no phone number. We remembered that he was very friendly with Police Inspector Turner. I eventually found him at Maidstone Police Headquarters, gave him the news, asked him to let Royston know, and asked him to get Royston to phone me. It was 24 hours before I received his call and unfortunately too late for him to go with Pattie. She took one of her friends with her. It must have been very hard as she was expecting her first child, who was born in September 1989, and named Nathan Christopher. The funeral took place in Florida at Winter Park Cemetery.

Life carried on in our new house/bungalow at Station Road, Teynham. Before Roger was killed, I had talked to him about going to Alaska and asked if he would like to come. I can always remember his reaction: 'Too true! It's somewhere I have always wanted to go. If you do that, then I will take you to New England in the autumn, when all the trees are showing their different colours'. Unfortunately, it did not happen with him, but Anne and I went later on and pretended he was with us.

Our Alaska trip was quite eventful. Pat, Royston's wife, made all the arrangements as she was running a small travel agent, and she managed to get us a good deal. We flew to Vancouver, then on to Prince Rupert, where we boarded a cruise liner, and sailed up what is known as the Inner Passage, which very narrow. We stopped at two ports, but we didn't get off. It was Skagway, which I was looking forward to seeing; this was where the Klondike Gold Rush started in the late1800s.

I had seen it on TV, when thousands of men, women and children went there to start a pilgrimage to Dawson City, many miles further north into Canada. The route goes through the mountains with tracks that are only 2 feet wide in places. They would buy goods at Skagway, and those who could afford it, would buy a donkey. Apparently, there was a man, called Smith, who was later shot and buried near the railway which was built later. Smith and his cronies controlled everything in Skagway. The next stop for the gold searchers was Whitehorse, where, again, they could replenish their stock. This was the last place where they could do this, and they still had a long way to go. Skagway is like going back in time, with wooden walkways, old houses and photos showing the mud roads with the tree stumps, although now there are many new properties, cafés, bars and hotels. I chose one of the oldest hotels in which to stay. Anne was not impressed, but agreed to try it only on the condition that if she didn't like it, we would find somewhere more modern.

Well, it was as if you were back in the 1800s and I was smitten. We walked up a steep stairway, just like the ones you see in the old films when fighting breaks out, and someone is thrown down it. The bedroom door was old and crooked, and it creaked when opened. The floor was also uneven, making walking interesting. There was an iron bedstead, with a hard mattress, but all the bed linen was very crisp and clean. There was also a table and chair in the room; both were very unstable.

We had been in bed for about two hours when there was a bang on the door and someone shouting 'Police!'. I must admit, it put the wind up me. The first thing that went through my mind was what have I could have done wrong, but nothing came to mind. I opened the door and there was a policeman standing in front of me. He asked if I was Mr Figg, I told him I was and he gave me a telephone number to call. Looking at it, I knew it was not a English number, but it was only when I went downstairs that I was told it was a Florida number; that meant it could only be from Royston. It turned out that Christopher had been admitted to St Thomas' Hospital in London for a kidney transplant, something he had been waiting for years. We got the phone number of the hospital and phoned him. It was rather funny: we spoke to the nurse and told her we the parents of Christopher Figg, and that we were speaking from Alaska. Apparently, she ran into his ward shouting Chris your mother and father are on the phone from Alaska, and when everybody heard her, they gave a great cheer. We offered to come back home, but the nurse and Chris said not to and that we should carry on with our trip, as there was nothing we could do. They told us to visit on our return, as he would be in hospital for another three weeks, so we did as we were told.

Chris arrived back home the following week and started looking around for a job. It was wonderful to see him looking better and getting out enjoying life again, having a drink with his mates and so on. It was then that he met a young chap, by the name of Kevin Chapman, who was trying to make a living from landscaping. He had a small office at the Norton Garden Centre Teynham Apparently, he knew a surveyor that worked for the construction company, Wiltshire, and they were doing some hospital building work for the South East Health Service. Unfortunately, because he wasn't a registered landscape contractor with them, he was unable to tender for the work. Chris offered to help him, by getting me involved, so I did, but it was only to try and use my influence within the Landscape Department of the NHS. Within three weeks, I had him registered and got him the work, on the promise that I would supervise it. This meant that I was back working again, but at least Chris was doing something, and again, work came in thick and fast. I could only use my name for tendering and signing letters, though. I had sold the name AE Figg & Son to Paul Figg, together with the company.

So we named our company Creative Landscape. Chris's friend's father now came in with a £5000 loan and a bank guarantee up to £20,000. Chris had no money, and I would not put money into it unless his father did, but then I only paid out if we were short of ready cash and I would take it out as soon as possible. I also worked free of charge, except for petrol, for a year, when I expect the business to be on its feet.

Now Chris' friend, Kevin Chapman, wanted more money for himself, but I was not taking any money out of the business and Chris and Wendy,were managing on his income. As with any small business, using borrowed money, you have to forget about increased wages until you have a sound balance sheet. I tried to explain this, but his father agreed with his son, saying 'we should pay everyone a ten percent increase, as we are making money'. I told them that, in that case, I was not prepared to carry on, unless I was also paid, and I knew what that would mean. As winter came, and work slowed down owing to weather conditions and such, we would be back to square one. Then when the spring came, we would need more money and more labour to cope with the incoming work, but nobody would listen. Of course, it happened, and Kevin's father had to go to the bank and borrow more money. Eventually money become increasingly difficult and the company ceased trading.

It was now 1996/7 and Anne found it was getting more difficult to go up and down the stairs. We all thought it was arthritis, little did we know it was the start of the deterioration of her health. So we decided to sell the house in Station Road, Teyham, and try and buy a bungalow somewhere near Canterbury, but it proved much more difficult than we thought. It wasn't until 2000, that Anne found what she wanted. Unfortunately it wasn't in a very good state, and it needed a lot of money spending on it. In the meantime, property prices started to collapse, and before we realised it, £30,000 was wiped off the value of the house we were selling. I had put the house on the market in 1999 and had several viewers and offers, but nowhere near the price I wanted, and it had now become a buyers' market. It was mid 2000 when a foreign gentleman and his partner came knocking on the door. He said that the paper-shop owner had told him that the house was for sale and he asked if could they look round. I'm always suspicious when this sort of thing happens, I am not a racist, but when he mentioned he came from Nigeria, that set the bells ringing; they are well-known for trying to get something for nothing. I knew I had to be one step ahead of him, particularly as he was well-spoken and very charming. He had money in Nigeria, but had difficulties in getting it out, and it would be six months before he would be able to get the funds released. He said his partner would help him. Apparently she had many contacts in the Nigerian government, so we agreed on a price, and I insisted on a deposit of ten percent which was none returnable. He asked me not to bank it until he gave me the word. I did warn him, however, that if he did not go through with the purchase, and I had not got my ten percent, then I would sue him; I had him tied up. I waited for six months before I phoned him, saying I was going to cash his cheque. In next to no time, he was at the door, asking me not to do that and saying he was sure he would have money within the next month. I wrote a letter out, and got him to sign it, stating that he intended to buy the property, and I also asked him for a further ten percent, so I two cheques now and a letter. He either had to buy the house, or lose his money, and at the worse I would bankrupt him. That put the wind up him, as that is the last thing he wanted, and I had a feeling he was in the country illegally.

In August 2000, I was informed that a bed was available in hospital for me to have a knee joint replacement. It was not the best timing for me and Anne as she was trying to find a bungalow near Canterbury and I was chasing to sell the house, but my right knee was getting so painful I had to go and get it done. It was mid-August before I could walk ,and then with two sticks, and during that time Anne found the bungalow, on Rough Common Road in Canterbury, where I am still living.

I was still putting great pressure on the prospective buyer of our house in Station Road, so I decided to bank the two cheques he had given me, knowing that perhaps they would not go through, but I hoping that they would. The cheques, unsurprisingly, were returned.

With this knowledge, I went berserk with him, and started to take proceeding's against him. Not only would I make him bankrupt, but he would also be charged for issuing cheques which he knew would not be honoured. If he was in the country illegally as well, then he was in deep trouble; he either had to come up with money, or go to prison and face possible deportation. Well that did the trick – within a week, the money was in my solicitor's hand. I made him wait to take possession until the property at Rough Common Road had been completely renovated, which was December 2000. Anne organised all the interior, with Chris helping where ever he could, and Daniel did all the work outside, with me supervising. God bless him, he worked like a Trojan, and without him, it would not only have taken much longer but would have been much more expensive. I was still having difficulties in getting about. After two more operations on one hip and the other knee (finally after eleven years), I can move around slowly with the help of a three-wheel walker. At least I can still get around and remain independent, and I can wash, shower and cook my own meals. Having turned 90 in 2010, I decided not to drive any more as it would not be fair on other people, even though I have all my faculties. Believe it or not, I can use a computer – it surprised me too – but life has been, and continues to be, good to me; it has enabled me to do lots of other things.

When we moved into Rough Common Road, I was lost to know what to do with my time. I always used to look forward to the day I could retire, but it was not as easy as I thought. After working sometimes twelve to eighteen hours a day, not just physically but mentally as well, to try and build up savings that would to enable us to have a reasonable standard of living, it can be difficult to stop working. Anne was still very much involved in the Royal British Legion, she had now become President of the Kent Women's Section. In early 2004, she was presented with the MBE by Prince Charles at Buckingham Palace, for her work on the War Pension Committee and working with the war widows through The Royal British Legion. After Anne's death in July 2005, Anne Widdecombe MP replaced her as the president.

[*Christopher, Anne, Albert, Annette MBE*]

To keep myself occupied, I bought two greenhouses and started to grow my own bedding plants. I already had the front garden re-laid. There was no lawn, I didn't want the problem of mowing, so it was all planted out with roses, bedding plants and ground cover. I joined the Normandy Veterans Association in Canterbury and the Market Garden Association, and was soon voted onto the committee.

If you'll pardon the expression, I've jumped the gun a little there, so let me take you back a few decades. It was sometime in 1960 that I was told by one of our regiment's men (Syd Sharp) who lived near Teynham, that the regiment (112 Field Artillery) had formed an 'Old Comrades Association', something I knew nothing about. I was posted away from the regiment in 1945, but Syd had been to one dinner and people were asking if anyone knew where Bert Figg lived. It was then that Syd contacted me. Unfortunately at the time, I could not afford to go, as money was short. Six years later, in 1966, I went to my first dinner in London. By chance, my son, Roger, was in London Docks, so I took him along with me, that was a mistake. He was asking everyone what I was like as a sergeant, and of course everyone was telling him I was a real hard bugger, and quite a few of them had been put on a charge by me, which had resulted in them being confined to the barracks for seven days. I continued to go to the dinners, and at times I took Anne, along with my daughter Annette.

In 1998, whilst at one of these dinners, one of our ex-officers, Dougie Goddard announced that the 43rd Wessex Division had formed an association for all members, and he urged us to join, which I did. He also informed us that they had hoped to sponsor some trees to be planted at an Arboretum, which was being planned in Derbyshire, in memory of all the service personnel who died in WW2. They were unable to do this, though, owing to the lack of funds, so I offered to find the trees free of charge from nurseries that I had dealt with, during my time in business. Apparently, they also had to find £10,000 to buy the site, which was beyond their capability, so the whole idea fell through.

In early 1998, I was watching a TV program called Animal Park, which was filmed at Longleat in Wiltshire. The owner was the Marquis of Bath, who was a charming man, well-known for his womanizing' he called his women 'wifelets'. He had several children by them, and he provided for all of them. He was married, but his wife lived in France, she kept a very tight rein on his expenses, and was very much involved with the running of the Estate. She used to visit twice a year to make sure all was well, but never worried about his philandering, he was only doing what the old kings of England had done. Over the years, since it opened in 1966, Longleat built up a whole range of wild animals, and the very grand house, full of the Marquis' extraordinary murals was open to the public. It was the first safari park of its kind outside of Africa, and thousands of people visit each year.

It was whilst watching the program, that the idea of an alternative location for a plantation of trees, in memory of the 43rd Wessex Division, came to mind. I thought if the 43rd Wessex Division Association could not afford to plant at the new arboretum, then we would have our own; I was sure I could get it done at no charge and all sponsored. I had no idea that this would start a rollercoaster of projects over the years. After a very short period of deliberating, I picked up the phone, rang the Longleat office and spoke to the secretary, explaining to her what I wanted to do. She advised me to write to the Marquis, with as much detail as possible, just as I had explained to her, and she would make sure it was put in front of him. She also asked if I was sure I could make it work, as they received many requests for different projects every year, but very few were ever completed. I assured her that indeed I could.

I sat down and compiled a letter as she advised, and this was something I had never done before, but I was full of confidence that I could make it work. Within a week, I had a letter back saying that we could have a piece of land opposite an old WW2 pillbox. How apt that was; they had taken my suggestion very seriously and had put a lot of thought into it, themselves. For those who may not be familiar with a 'pillbox', I will explain. During WW2, there was a real worry that the Germans would try to invade Britain. With this in mind, defences were built all around the country, and they were very varied in their design and use. The most basic was a small concrete building with several sides. It had gun portals to allow soldiers to fire their rifles and machine guns through. These pillboxes were placed at strategic positions covering road junctions, bridges, canals and other locations thought to be at risk. Fortunately, they were never used in anger, but many remain as silent sentinels of a bygone time.

Now back to Longleat. After receiving the offer of this piece of land, I contacted the secretary of the association, Bill Edwards, who at the time I had never met. I had only been in the association six months, having joined as a life member, and he only knew me as a new comer. I mentioned the arboretum, and his immediate reply was that we were unable to afford it, I said I knew, but asked if the association would accept the offer of a plantation of forty-three trees, on a piece of ground in Longleat Park? He nearly exploded, shouting 'I just told you we can't afford it, and in any case how are you going to get permission and are you going to pay for it? Don't waste my time'. I thought to myself, 'we've got a right pessimist here'. I managed to get another few words in by saying I had already been offered the ground in front of a WW2 pillbox, and after a few minutes of talking, he asked how I had managed sort it all. My simple answer to that was, 'I ask the Marquis of Bath and he said that he was delighted to do it. All I had to do was supply the trees and his staff would plant, stake and tie them and then maintain them for life'. I was all ready for the next question from Bill, which was 'who is paying for the trees?' My answer was I that I would get them donated by nurseries, in the Wessex area, that I had done business with when I ran my own landscaping company, for many years. 'okay,' he said, 'so what about a memorial stone and suitable plaque?' The Marquis of Bath had told me that he would arrange for Yeoman Quarry to supply a suitable piece of stone at no charge, and that he would also provide a plaque, engraved with the wording provided by the association. There was nothing else to add, other than telling Bill that I would be at the AGM in Exeter in May (1998), after I had had a meeting with Longleats' estate manager to sort out the details. Then I would be in a position to give the meeting more details. There was a hundred percent approval at the meeting for the plans.

In August 1998, Bill phoned me asking if I had ever been on Hill 112 where the 43rd Wessex Memorial stood. Although I had heard of its existence, having fired hundreds of shells on it in July 1944, in support of our infantry. I had never been there in person, and at the time thought it was named after my regiment, 112 Field Regiment Royal Artillery. I was at least three or four miles behind the infantry. We were in comparative safety, and I have always thought how lucky I was joining the artillery and not the infantry – if I had, I probably would not be writing this now. I had to inform Bill that I had never been, so he invited me together with another three ex-infantry men, to go with them in September 1998. Of course, I jumped at the chance to see the hill I had fired on from Carpique Airport, and remembering the words I said to my gunners at the time. We had been firing on it day after day and in the end I remarked to them 'I wondered what the hell the infantry are up to, let us get up there we will move the bastards!' I had no idea what our lads were going through.

It was whilst on our journey, that Bill and the others told me all about the battle, and the amount of casualties that the division suffered during the twelve to fourteen days of fighting. Being so far back in our gun pits, we knew nothing of what was happening in front of us. All we knew was that we were firing like hell, hoping that we were helping them. I have no idea how many Germans I killed with my gun, but it must have been in the hundreds, perhaps thousands in the eleven months of fighting between 1944 and 45. I'm glad that I don't know.

We arrived on Hill 112, and I was amazed at the wide open countryside that surrounded it, though it really didn't seem much of a hill. There were only a few hedgerows to shelter from enemy fire - apparently in 1944 it was all cornfields, with a small wood in the centre, which become known as Cornwall Wood, after the Duke of Cornwall Light Infantry who lost a lot of men trying to captured it. I stood in front of the emorial and I could see myself on my gun again, repeating the words 'what the hell are they up to?' I realised how stupid I had been back then, and it brought tears to my eyes. To really understand just what went on, and the bloodshed, you need to read the book Hill 112 by Tim Saunders. published by Pen and Sword.

It was whilst there, on the hill, that another gentleman came and spoke to Bill and the others. I was introduced to him by saying 'this is Albert Figg, it is his first time on the hill, he was a sergeant gunner, a five-mile sniper'. His name was Fred Morcel, and he had escaped from Jersey in 1939/40, aged just sixteen, and joined the Free French Forces. The talking went on for a few minutes and then Fred asked Bill when they were going to get a memorial tank to go on the hill The usual pessimistic answer of 'we can't do it' followed. Bill explained that they had been trying for the last five years, and had been unable to find one, unless they could find £10,000? Now bearing in mind I had just got approval to plant forty-three trees at Longleat, the other chap with us, Frank Greggs, jumped in and said 'Albert, you can do this.' The usual answer from Bill was 'Don't be daft Frank, if we are unable to do it, how in the hell can Albert do it?' Suddenly, I could feel the stares of Fred, Bill and Frank looking at me. At this point, I was wondering what the hell they were talking about a tank for, until it was explained to me that hundreds of our tanks were lost in the battle, and most of the crews burnt to death. The local people in the area of Cote (Hill) 112, and its association, wanted to put a memorial tank on the space they had left, alongside their own memorial on the hill.

On our way home I asked Bill who they had approached about this tank. He answered 'Everybody, including the Tank Museum! We've been told it's almost impossible to find an old WW2 tank, and if we did it would cost a lot of money, so forget about it, Albert. Don't waste your time, you will never find one'. Of course, I couldn't forget it. Anne kept saying to me 'Go on, you can do it', and this was in September/October 1998. The annual dinner and AGM of our 'Old Comrades Association' was held on the first Saturday of November, and I am not sure how it all happened, but all of a sudden, I heard one of our members, ex-officer Dougie Goddard, mention my name. It was unusual to hear your name being discussed between ex-officers, but apparently he knew about the forty-three tree plantation that I had organized at Longleat, and also that I was going to get a tank for Hill 112. A cheer went up and everybody was clapping. I had not said anything to anybody about the tank, I'd only told Anne. Apparently, Frank Griggs, one of the men with me on Hill in September, had been telling everyone that Albert Figg was going to do it. I had to tell them that I had not promised to do anything, only that I would think about it.

Anne was at the dinner with me, and afterwards she said that I would have to do it now. It was whilst at the dinner that my mind was working on another idea. Everything had been organised for the tree-planting the following year, but one thing I kept thinking about, was that our OCA did not have a standard, whereas most other associations had one. This seemed the perfect time to propose one, as all the members had been cheering and clapping. I told them that if we could raise £500, we could buy one, and carry it with pride at the dedication of the tree plantation, in May 1999. The room went very quiet, with exception of one person, the secretary ,Wilf Blackwell, who thought it was a good idea. Without hesitation, I said 'you've had your hands out of your pockets, now's the chance to put them back in again, but instead of buying drinks, all of you can put a fiver on the table'. Of course, they had a job to refuse, especially when Wilf and I put our fivers on the table, and the rest had to follow our lead. We were on a roll, and within ten minutes we had £300, reaching our target of £500 within a month.

With news out that I was going to find a tank for Hill 112, I thought 'how in the hell am I going to do this, where do I start, who do I ask?' I did everything I could think of, like phoning the Tank Museum, tank firing ranges, tank associations, and so on, but with no luck. Things were looking very gloomy, and I was beginning to get very despondent, feeling that I would not be able to do it. I remember thinking that I had achieved a lot since coming home in 1946, and I was not going to be beaten by this.

In1999 I saw an advert in the Kent Messenger, saying that there was a man travelling to Belgium, who would be prepared to take a wreath from anyone who would like to have it laid on a grave in any cemetery, on route. He belonged to the Invicta Military Preservation Society and the Military Vehicle Trust. The members of both these clubs restore ex-military vehicles, which include WW2 vehicles ranging from guns, tanks, Jeeps, trucks, motorbikes and anything in between. Once restored, they display them at different shows all around the country, raising money for charities. So I phoned him, thinking he might have some idea where I could get a tank. His response was that he would send me the MVT magazine called *Windscreen* and perhaps I would find one in there. He also told me to contact Mr Rex Cadman, who might be able to help. He was a member of the IMPS and organised The War and Peace show, something I had never heard of before. When I spoke to Rex, his reply could not have been more discouraging. 'What, you're looking for a tank? Have you got £10,000 to spare, because that is what it will cost you, you must be crazy to think someone will give you one!' Unfortunately that is *just* what I was hoping.

The next morning, I received the promised MVT magazine. Whilst looking through it, unable to find a tank for sale or otherwise, I noticed that there were branches of the MVT all around the country. I decided that I would compile a letter and send it to each branch… eventually I managed to do this, after several attempts all in long hand, but my writing is not very good. I got Annette to correct it, and she typed it up for me (this was before I could use a computer. I didn't learn to use one until 2005).

That was all well and good, but then I needed more copies, so I bought a secondhand photocopier, paper, envelopes and stamps. Suddenly, the cost began to spiral, but it spurred me on. I was getting more and more determined that I would get this tank, but the problem was how to do it.

I sent the thirty letters, and then it was a case of waiting. Two weeks went by, and I heard nothing from anyone, so I went back to *Windscreen* magazine again, to see if I could find anyone else who might be able to help. I found the name of Simon Johnson, an MVT committee member, so I thought I'd try him… if you don't ask, you never get anything! In less than a week, he replied, saying 'so you're the Albert Figg who has been writing to branch members. They have been in contact with me, asking who is this Albert Figg character, and what is he trying to do?' I phoned Simon, at the time he worked for the BBC in Manchester, and I told him I was trying to find a tank to go on Hill 112, as a memorial to all the tank crews who died during the battle in June/July 1944. There was silence from the other end of the phone, and after a couple of seconds he started to tell me the story of his father who took part in the battle as a tank commander in the Royal Scots Greys. That, of course, got him talking about what he knew of the Hill and the battle to capture it. He started to quiz me and asked if I had served in tanks? And if not tanks which unit? I replied that I was not in tanks, but I was a sergeant field gunner on 25-pounders, a Five Mile Sniper. He wanted to know why I was doing this and so I replied that it was fifty-five years ago when it happened, and nobody else has bothered about it. I told him that the Association Cote (Hill) 112 and my 43rd Wessex Division Association, who were in Operation Jupiter, had been trying for the last five years without any luck and so I had taken up the challenge.

After a long conversation about what would be a good representative tank to go on the hill, we felt that perhaps a British Churchill tank would be the most appropriate. Simon then asked me if I could write a letter, explaining what I was trying to achieve, and send it to him. He said he would then forward it on to all the BBC local radio stations, all forty of them, as they would all be interested in doing something about my challenge. It was the end of April 1999, and I was aiming to get one on the Hill by the 10th of July (the 55th Anniversary of Operation Jupiter). At the same time, in early May, I had a phone call from Chris Davis, an MVT member in Southampton who thought he had found a tank in a scrap yard and wanted to know if would I go and see it, which I did. Although it was only going to cost £200, there was far too much work to do on it, and would cost a lot of money, so that was a wasted journey.

I must now return to autumn 1998, when I bought the OCA standard. I was hastily reminded by my wife, Anne, that all standards have to be dedicated in church by a vicar, before they can be displayed. It was a Royal Artillery standard, and I thought it was only fitting for it to be dedicated in the Royal Artillery Garrison Church, at the School of Artillery, at Lark Hill in Salisbury, Wiltshire. I knew nobody at the school, after all these years, so the only thing for it was to go there, and bluff my way in to see someone with authority. The regimental sergeant major seemed to be the best choice, so I set off; I knew where the barracks were, having been there many times on courses during the war. On arrival, I was instructed by the guard to go and report to guard house. Over the years I have become a bit of a joker, it helps to break the ice, and 99 percent of the time it has helped me to get what I wanted. So, into the guard house I marched, stood to attention in front of the sergeant of the guard, and announced myself as 890390 Sergeant Figg of the 112 Field Regiment, here to give myself up as a deserter since 1944. The sergeant nearly fell over, saying 'you'd better see the captain', so off we go to see him. I told him the same story, of course, and he looked up at me and started laughing and asking how old I was. 'Seventy-eight, Sir,' was my reply. The captain turned to the guard sergeant, saying that he thought I was is having him on, and they both laughed their heads off. It worked, because the captain then asked me what it was I was after. I told him about the standard, and he said that I'd come to the wrong barracks and that I needed RSM Adler further up the road at the school.

I had gone to wrong place! The captain did say that if I went there, with my story of the standard, that I would get what I wanted, so with much thanks to him, I went a few hundred yards up the road. I saw the guard commander, who had a grin on his face, so I could only assume he had been told to expect me, and that I wanted to see RSM Adler. In normal circumstances, they would escort unknown people to his office, but this time, he told me where to go, saying, 'just up the road you will see a twenty-five pounder gun outside and you can park your car the other side of the road. I found the twenty-five pounder, without any difficulty, and parked the car. I walked to the office, full of trepidation, for standing at the door was the orderly sergeant, who wanted to know what I wanted. I told him I wanted to see the RSM, and he asked if I had got an appointment. Before I could answer, the RSM shouts out 'who is it sergeant?' and he responds 'Oh it's a gentleman who is asking to see you sir.' 'Well show him in' says the RSM. I went in, stood to attention and said '890390 Sergeant Figg reporting for duty after going absent without leave in 1944, sir'. I can remember the look on his face and hoping he would smile, but I could never remember an RSM smiling during the whole of my time in the army ,and he did not let me down now. There was not a hint of a smile on his face. He asked me what I wanted, and I explained that I wanted to get a standard dedicated at the garrison church for my 112 Field Regiment, Royal Artillery Old Comrades Association. I explained that I had recently raised the money and purchased it, and to encourage him to agree, I told him that the master gunner of the Royal Artillery, Major General Ferndale, plus many high ranking officers such as brigadiers, colonels and civil dignitaries, like the Mayor of Swindon would be coming. The ultimate aim, of course, was also that we hoped to carry it at the dedication of the tree-planting and memorial to the 43rd Wessex Division in May. 'Okay,' he said, 'can you let me have all details in writing, and include anything else you might like us to help you with'. But still no smile. I couldn't help it then, and I said, 'you old bugger, none of you RSM's smile! With that, he had a little grin on his face, as he shouted to the orderly sergeant, 'escort Mr Figg to the sergeant's mess, and give him dinner. Then, you can take the rest of the day off, and show him around all the new types of equipment we use today'. That was a day I shall never forget.

My motto worked again, if you don't ask you don't get. But when I made contact with the Mayor of Swindon's office and spoke to his secretary, she could not understand why I would want the mayor to attend a dedication of a standard to the Royal Artillery, asking what it had got to do with Swindon? I was dumbstruck, and I must admit I was getting a bit angry. Didn't she know that Swindon had its own regiment, the 112 Field Regiment Royal Artillery, that trained in 1938, and that the regiment was made up of men from Swindon and the surrounding area. The regiment was stationed at Prospect Place, Prospect Hill in Swindon and served all through the Normandy Campaign. She claimed she knew none of this, as she was born after the war. 'But you must have records somewhere in Swindon,' I said, 'have a word with the Swindon Advertiser, they produced an article in May 1945 telling Swindon of the actions we had been in.' I then asked if she would now please speak to the mayor and ask him if he would come as a representative of Swindon. I was rather naughty, because I continuing to say that if he could not come, then I would put an article in the paper saying that the Mayor of Swindon wasn't prepared to recognise the Swindon Artillery Regiment and the men who lost their lives. He agreed to come.

The letter was duly sent to RSM Adler, including a few extras such as asking if two twenty-five pounder guns could be put on display. I asked if he could personally take the parade and told him that there be ten senior NCO's in attendance. Finally, I asked if the colonel of the school would also like attend. He agreed, and everything was set for May,1999. Just before the dedication at Longleat, another gentleman from the MVT said he thought he had found a tank, and he would be able tell me more at the dedication. This raised my spirits. It was May, and I still wanted to get one on the Hill for July the 10th, the 55th anniversary of the battle. Unfortunately, this second tank, turn out to be the same tank I'd turned down earlier on, so that was another disappointment and we were back to square one. The dedication took place, and then a march past by all the veterans. There were about two hundred of us all together, and a military band with Lord Bath taking the salute. There was then a military musical concert, with me being invited to join Lord Bath, up the steps, on the saluting base. Unfortunately, I have no picture of that, but there is one of me standing behind the memorial stone.

It was whilst at Longleat, that Brigadier, Tony Faith, came up to me asking if I had found a tank. I must have sounded a little disappointed when I said no, because his words were 'don't worry, you will do it, and when you do, let me know, and I will donate £500 out of the 43rd Wessex Brigade fund.' Without me knowing, that one little remark seemed to set things going.

A couple of days afterwards, I received a phone call from Roger Phillips of BBC Radio Merseyside. Apparently they had received the letter from Simon Johnson telling them I was looking for a tank. 'Is that Albert Figg,' he asked, 'is it a water tank you are looking for?' 'No,'I told him, 'It's WW2 Churchill tank with a gun on it.' I think I took the wind out of his sails, because it took several seconds before he answered. 'Do you mean one of those big ones that was in the war? My God, that is the first time we have ever been ask for one of those.' I then explained why I wanted one, and that I was a Normandy veteran who wanted to put it on Hill 112 in Normandy, as a memorial to all the tank crews who'd lost their lives during the battle, fifty-five years ago. His reply was, 'hold on a minute, and I will put you through to our A-Team.' I thought this was a joke, as the A-team was a film and television series where the goodies always beat the baddies, but a lady came on the phone saying she understood I was looking for a big tank with a gun on it do you know where we can start to find one? I told her 'Yes, by telling your listeners about it, as somebody listening might have a suggestion. There are hundreds of veterans out there who took part in the battle for Hill 112 during Operation Epsom and Jupiter, in the summer of 1944. The division I was in, the 43rd Wessex, had 7000 casualties in nineteen days.' Sp she agreed to see what they could do.

About ten minutes later, the phone rang again, and I heard this voice say, 'this is Roger Phillips, at BBC Radio Merseyside.' Unknown to me, he was on air, and he was telling his audience that he had a Normandy veteran on the phone and that he would like them to listen to his story. 'Hello Albert Figg, are you there? Please tell the listeners what you are trying to do?' I was gobsmacked. Me, speaking live on the radio. It took me several seconds before I could speak. I needed a little prompting from Roger. 'Come on Albert, now's your chance, so tell the people exactly what you have told me.' After gathering myself together, I started to talk, and as a lot of people who know me are too well aware, once I start, I have a job to stop. Roger let me go on for a good ten minutes, after which he asked, 'do you think you will have to pay for one?' 'I hope not,' I replied 'but I have been told it will cost up to £10,000, which will mean I will have to start asking for donations.' 'Right,' he said, 'let us know if you find the tank, and in the meantime, we will ask around to see what we can do.'

Shortly after this, I received another phone call, this time from BBC Radio Kent asking if I would be interested in speaking on their radio station, and telling their listeners about the memorial tank. As you might have gathered, I am not one to miss an opportunity if it is going to help raise the money required. The next morning I received a call from the secretary of the London branch of the Royal Tank Association, David Francis. He asked if it was true about the memorial tank, and wanted to know if he and two other members come and see me? 'Yes, of course', was my reply. I think they thought it was a joke, and they could only be sure by seeing and speaking to me. You have to remember, it was fifty-five years after the battle, and nobody had ever thought about doing it, and now, to rub salt into the wound, here comes a Royal Artillery chap to do it for them. After the meeting, they were convinced of what I was trying to achieve, and I was invited to go along to their next meeting in London, to explain to their members why I was doing this. It was whilst at the meeting that I received a cheque for £150 from them, and also at the same time, that I was made a honourary member of the RTR.

The following day, I received another phone call from a chap callled Carl Brown from Aylesbury, in Buckinghamshire. Carl said 'I understand you are looking for a old WW2 Churchill tank?' 'Yes,' was my reply, 'but how did you find out?' It turned out that a friend of his heard me speaking on BBC Radio Merseyside and remembered that he had one, but it needed to be restored, costing a total of £9,000 plus VAT. To start the ball rolling He needed £1,000 up front to get it off the field, but when I asked him where it was, but he said he was unable to tell you me that. 'I'm sorry, ' I said 'but I have got no money at the moment. I will come back to you as soon as I have.' I don't know why I said that, as I had no idea where the money would come from.

The story now becomes even more unbelievable, but it is neverthless true. The following day, I received a phone call from Dougie Goddard, saying he had a very wealthy friend who was an ex-lieutenant colonel of the Engineers. He had been in the 43rd Wessex Division in charge of the Engineers when bringing the Paras back from Arnhem. 'If it is money you need, ' said Dougie, 'he would like to help. He'll be waiting in his office for you to phone him.' I phoned him straight away, saying I had been told that he would like to help me with finances for a tank. 'Yes, indeed' was his reply, 'find one and let me know.' I told him I'd already found one, but I needed a £1000 to secure the tank and to get it off the ground,into the workshop for repair. 'Right ,'he said '£1000 will be in the post tonight, and let me know where the workshop is, because I would like to see it.'

The news of the tank got around the country fast. The next person to phone was Rex Cadman 'You're a lucky bugger,' he said 'I hear you've found a tank, but you've still got to find £10,000, how are you going to that?' Not knowing, or having even met the man, I asked how he'd found out? 'That is for me to know, and you to find out', was his reply, 'but I would like to meet you. I will send you a ticket to come to our War and Peace show in July.' I'd never heard of it, but I was about to find out just how important a show it was. Rex said 'come along you just never know what will happen, you might even find someone who will help you'. That was the beginning of a very long friendship, even to this day (July 2011).All this activity surrounding the tank happened in one week at the end of May/beginning of June 1999.

The next day, I received another phone call from Simon Johnson of MVT, saying the Trust's committee had agreed to give me £1500 towards the tank. We have already heard that you have found a suitable example with Carl Brown; he is one of our members. The next phone call was from the chairman of the Southampton branch, offering £1000 and a loan of £1500 if required. Another £500 came from the 43rd Wessex Brigade (Brigadier Tony Faith). I phoned BBC Radio Merseyside and told Roger Phillips that I had found a tank, thanks to them, and asked if I could speak to the A team and thank them, which I duly did. At the same time, I gave them the phone number of Carl Brown, and told them the cost of it. I asked if they would phone him to see if they could get him to reduce the cost, but said that I would be keen to talk to him, on air, to explain how he had come to my help. After all, it was going to be a memorial to all those tankies who had lost their lives for the freedom he has today. It worked becaus he reduced the price by £500 and agreed to pay the VAT. That was great! I had got the tank for £8,500. In total, so far with the £500 from Tony Faith, 43rd Wessex Brigade, I had now got £4000 plus the £1500 on loan if required it, I was on a roll, or so I thought.

The money started coming in, in varying amounts, from a few pounds up to £10's, 20's, £100 and £500 from all over the country. By mid-June, 1999, three weeks after I started, I had raised £5,500. Carl told me that he would require a further £4000 on top of my initial £1000 making a total of £5000, and once he had restored it he would require the balance of £3,500 within three months. It is at this point I dropped the bombshell on him, saying that I wanted it ready to go up on Hill112 on the 9th July 1999, ready for the fifty-fifth anniversary of the battle. He reaction of horror was only natural, as he pointed out that it only gave him four weeks to finish it. I apologized, but I had already told everybody it would be there, so I'm afraid he had to get move on.

The 43rd Wessex Association was going to hold their memorial service on the hill on the 10th July, but the secretary, Bill Edwards, refused to accept that I had even got a tank, or that it would be on the Hill for the 10th July. As a result, he made no attempt to include it in the memorial service. Typical of Bill, if he could not do it then how could anybody else?

A big shock awaited me, just round the corner. I had been so busy and excited at getting so much money in that I had forgotten two very important factors. The first one was how was I going to get the Churchill over to Normandy in time, and the secondd and probably more important factor, was what would it cost? The question had been put to me by the colonel from London, who gave me the first £1000, and I had to admit it was something that I had not really thought about. He told me not to worry about it, but to contact him when the time came to take the tank over to France and Hill 112, so that is exactly what I did. That afternoon, I had a call from Carl Brown, saying he had got a chap, called Captain Bowler, who wanted to speak to me. Captain Bowler started by saying that he understood that I had a tank and wanted it transporting to Normandy. I told him that was correct and asked him who he was and how he could help. His reply was a total shock, as he explained he was a captain in the Logistic Corps, and one of his jobs was to arrange transport for such things. He added that he had been instructed by his CO to help me in any way he could. What a turn up this was, but when this sort of luck happens, there is often a 'but' involved, and this was no exception. Unfortunately, most of the tank transporters were in Kosovo, except one, but it was in the depot and needed repairing. I told you there is always a 'but'. Nevertheless, Captain Bowler said he was in the process of getting the spare parts, and it should be ready on the 8th July 1999. It would be tight to get the tank onto Hill112 on the 9th ready for the 55th anniversary of the battle of the 10th, but it might just be possible.

This was around the first of July, and I was also assured that the tank would be ready in time. I remember sitting down and thinking that the

Lord must be with me. But I had spoken too soon, as another bombshell hit me. The next question was which ship is was going on and from which port? Also, we needed authorisation from the French authorities to take it, and six soldiers onto French soil. It hadn't crossed my mind, and all of a sudden, everything was going down the drain, or so I thought. I had to say to the captain that I would need to get back to him on those final points. In spite of my little faith, right out of the blue, I got another phone call from the colonel. He had been in touch with the CO Logistic Corps, and was told of my problems. He was definitely my guardian angel as once again, he said that I didn't need to worry, and that he would sort it out as he had friends in the French Embassy and the military. He said 'just tell me what day the tank will be going and to which port in Normandy. I will also phone P&O Ferries and get a price and I will pay for it.' Amazingly, by 4th July everything was in place. The colonel had spoken to P&O, and the cost of transport was £1000, sailing from Portsmouth. I felt that P&O was charging the going rate, and had not taken into account that it was a memorial tank, so I phone Brittany Ferries also in Portsmouth. I explained what it was all about and asked if they could help. They came back saying they could do it for £500 with also free meals for the six soldiers and me, providing they could take a photo when the tank was being loaded, for their own publicity. I phoned the Colonel saying I had got the price down to £500 from Brittany Ferries, and his reply was, 'well done, Albert that was good initiative on your part, but I will send you the £1000, and you can put the rest into your tank fund.' It must all sound like a fairytale, but it is the honest truth and there's still more to come.

 I received a phone call, from Captain Bowler, saying that it was all set for the evening of the 8th July, 1999, and that I should be at Carl's yard by midday. The British Forces Television would be there to record the handover of the tank to me, the £4000 to Carl Brown, and the loading of it. All of this would then be broadcast to the forces around the world. Added to which, I was also to travel with them. Annette and Anne drove me to Aylesbury. It was about 1600hrs when we set off to Portsmouth, with the low loader transporter, a total weight 65 tonnes. We also had a spare towing vehicle, three Land Rovers and spare parts in case we had a break down There were the six soldiers, myself and Captain Bowler. As with all army movements, there are set rules whilst travelling on the public highway. You have to leave 60 yards between each vehicle, drive at a speed limit of 25 mph allowing the public to overtake and leave enough room for anyone to pull in front if needed. It was also broadcast on the radio that people driving on the A34 should be prepared for a long delay, owing to an army convoy on the road heading for Portsmouth. It said if you were in a hurry you should find another route. We stopped several times to check that the tank had not come loose, and also to let the travelling public past. Unfortunately, the transporter had a blowout on one of it tyres – you can imagine the problems that caused, a heavy-duty jack capable of lifting up 40 tonnes was needed. Normally, you would take the tank off and use the normal jack which they carried, but the Churchill was not in running condition, which meant it could not be removed from the trailer easily. This meant that Captain Bowler had to go to the Portsmouth Naval Base and get one from them. It was over two hours before we got moving again, and it was getting near the time to board the overnight ship at 2300hrs.

When we arrived, we found out we were going to have to wait until the morning and sail at 0600hrs. Apparently we were too heavy and there were too many vehicles, so this created a problem. All the military lads could get sleeping accommodation in the Navy barracks, but not me. It meant that I had to find a B&B, and at that time of the night, not knowing the place, I thought I would have to sleep in the Land Rover. Fortunately for us, there were two people who had been watching us coming down the A34, and had taken photos for the MVT magazine to show the members that the tank was actually on its way. It was amazing how many people thought that I would never achieve my mission; people have little faith, including myself at one stage. One of these two was called Craig White and he had heard the news of my predicament; he immediately offered to put me up for the night at his parent's house at Eastleigh six miles away. After a few minutes phoning his parents we were on our way. I will never forget the welcome they gave me, and to this day we are still very good friends.

After a few hours sleep I was delivered back to the docks. After all the private cars, foot passengers and light commercial vehicles had boarded we started loading. There were hundreds of people on the deck watching and cheering. They all knew what it was because Carl Brown had tied a large banner on the side that read 'This tank is a memorial for Hill 112 at the request of Albert Figg'. Once on board there were numerous people who wanted to speak to me, including Veterans of the 43rd, Wessex Division and tank regiments.

The crossing went well and we arrived at the port of Caen to a welcoming committee. The problem was (yes, another one) that I had told Bill Edwards, the Secretary of 43rd Association, that we would be arriving early morning. However, because of the delay in sailing, we didn't arrive until 1400hrs. Many of the 43rd Association members had arrived two days earlier on the 7th July, ready for the memorial service on the 10th, but of course I could not pass a message to Bill that we would be late and would not be there until the afternoon. They had apparently arrived on the Hill at 0900hrs and had waited until 1030hrs, when Bill announced that they would not wait any longer, and were going. He said it was all a hoax and that Albert hadn't got the tank in the first place so it was a waste of their time. Frank Griggs, however, was convinced that the tank would be coming. Gilles Osmond a member of the 112 Cote Association and a newcomer to the district, was in agreement with him. He insisted that the tank would be on the hill before the day was out. Frank and Gilles decided to phone the port. Gilles spoke to them, as Frank could not speak a word of French, and he was informed that the tank was on its way. It had been delayed because of its weight, and as a consequence it had been unable to sail on the original overnight crossing. They also told him that it was being brought over by Monsieur Albert Figg and they had a welcoming committee at the port waiting to greet him. This, of course was too late for Bill; he had left with all the others.

I shall never forget the big smile on Frank's face as we crept up the road towards the hill. He was standing in the middle of the road waving his arms, just like a little child, and was shouting to the rest of those who remained 'He's here! I knew you would not let us down Albert.' I hadn't let them down, and the Cote 112 Association started to open bottles of pink champagne. Everyone was over the moon, and congratulations were being offered by all; everybody seemed to have forgotten that the tank had to be taken off the lowloader. After about an hour, Captain Bowler reminded me that perhaps we ought to start thinking about unloading the tank. Everyone was having too much of a good time and wanted to continue with the celebrations. All the lads started moaning, saying 'we can wait a few more minutes'; they were enjoying themselves, with champagne flowing out of their ears. They'd never had it so good. With a little gentle persuasion, we turned our attention to the job in hand.

The unloading of a thirty-five tonne tank without an engine is no easy matter, but luckily, everybody knew what they were doing, as the transporter was reversed into position. Gently the trailer's wheels mounted the curb onto the newly laid footpath, where the wheels duly sunk in. A lot of repositioning of the trailer followed, until it was in the position we needed it. With the trailer now in position, the hydraulics on the trailer were used to raise one end, which allowed the tank to roll off with nothing else other than gravity to help it. However, because the wheel had sunk into the footpath, the tank would only run so far off and the hydraulics would not lift the low loader any higher. Fortunately for us, a local farmer was on hand, and he got his tractor hooked up to it, and pulled it into the exact position that I wanted it in, with the barrel of the gun pointing towards the wood over the far side of the field. We felt that this was fitting, as that was where a lot of the fighting took place and that is where the Churchill stands today. Hill 112 is on the D8 road, approximately 15 kilometres South West of Caen. When the tank was first placed, it was literally by the side of the main road, but since then a bypass has been built, and the tank and other memorials stand some 150 metres away.

After it was all over, I was taken by the troops to a French army barracks where we were stopping the night before the big day. The next day was the 10th July, 1999 and was the 43rd Wessex Division Association's parade and service of remembrance at the Wessex Memorial and the tank, on the same site. Poor old Bill was full of apologies when I arrived at the service with all the troops in full dress uniform. They had all worn overalls the day before, but they made sure they were well turned out for the parade. Bill walked over to me saying, 'right Albert, you're now going to lead the parade'. It was a great honour.

This was just one third of the work that had been done. I still had to raise the balance of the money which was £3,500. I had also inherited another job, unknown to me at the time. Like most things relating to standards and memorials, it had to be dedicated. However, because it was on French soil, and handed over to the Cote 112 Association, I thought that it could wait another year. That meant I could concentrate on raising the rest of the money first.

I arrived back home on the 11th July. A little money kept coming in, but not enough to fulfill the purchase price by the end of November. At a pinch, I could have borrowed the £1,500 offered by the MVT, leaving a balance of £2,000, which is still a large amount to raise. It was now the time to accept the invitation by Rex Cadman to meet him at the War and Peace Show. Knowing very little of what it was all about, I set off for the Hop Farm, Paddock-Wood, near Maidstone in Kent. It was about 1200hrs on a Saturday, and as I drew nearer to the place, the road was packed with traffic. On the opposite side of the road, I could see that Hop Farm was packed with tents and vehicles of all shape and sizes; it was unbelievable. It took nearly an hour to travel one mile to the entrance. When I eventually got there, I looked around and realised that I would not be able to walk around the showground – my knees used to hurt a lot – so I hired a scooter. If you have never been there then you should. It is the largest military vehicle show of its kind in Europe, if not the world. I started looking around until I came across a 25-pounder gun, similar to the one I used during the war. I found out that they fired it using a black powder-charged cartridge (no shell thankfully) at 1200hr each day, to start the show. Now that would bring back a few memories if I was able to fire it. It didn't take long for the decision to be made that I could fire it the following day.

[*REX CADMAN*]

Rex Cadman, the show organizer, was told about this and was in total agreement. The following day I was there well before time, and just before 1200hr an announcement was made over the loud speakers that for the first time since the end of the War an ex-gunnery sergeant of the Royal Artillery would be firing the gun. Good gracious, you never saw so many people running to the gun to take photos and asking me for my autograph – it was all rather embarrassing. It was about 1500hr when another announcement was made asking if I could make my way to the arena, as Mr Rex Cadman would like to meet me. I can tell you, going down the track to the main arena with people on either side clapping and cheering is very daunting. I eventually made it in to the arena where I was introduced to Rex.

[*ALBERT FIRING GUN*]

The announcer told the huge crowd that I was trying to raise money to pay for a memorial tank on Hill 112 Normandy. He turned to me, handed me his microphone and said 'here you are, Albert what would you like to say?' I'm not one to be lost for words, but have been on some occasions and this was one of them. With a little prompting, I started to tell the now silent crowd about the battle, and the huge amount of tanks that were lost, with most crews burnt to death. Out of the silence, someone shouted out 'yes, and my dad was one of them.' It was immediately after this, and rather amusingly, that the German re-enactment group took off their steel helmets and went around the spectators asking them to help me with a donation. Rex was so impressed with my determination that he had arranged this. Whilst all this was going on, tanks, guns and vehicles started to come into the arena and all lined up as though on parade. Everybody got out of their vehicles and stood in front of them. A Jeep came up to me and I was invited to climb aboard, to stand up in the front and take the salute, whilst the driver drove me along the line of parked vehicles, just like a general, inspecting his men. (If you look on the hill112 website, you will see a picture of me saluting). After I had inspected all vehicles, I was asked to present the prizes for the best turned-out vehicle in each of the different categories, such as gun, tank, and so on. I was given an honourary membership of the War and Peace Show, which gave me free entrance to the show for life.

It did not stop there. Rex had invited Anne, Annette and I to dinner the following night, at the Hop farm. It was a meal that he had organised to say thank you to all the volunteers who had helped in the organization and running of the show. When we arrived a table had been reserved in our name, the meal was a help-yourself affair and was very good. There was endless wine if you wanted it, and I suppose there must have been 50 or 60 people there. It must have been a hour or so after everybody had eaten, that Rex stood up thanked everyone for the work they had done and said how successful the show had been. He went on to say 'I have the pleasure to say that there was a gentleman and a veteran called Albert Figg here with us tonight.' He continued by saying 'most of you saw him fire the twenty-five pounder gun, and heard him speak in the arena. I am sure you were all impressed by the way he handled himself, and the thought he has for all his fallen comrades.' I thanked Rex for his kind words and then he said that a man was going to hand over a very heavy bag, to me, containing the money that was collected by the re-enactors in the arena the day before. It was placed on the table in front of me, which nearly collapsed under the weight. Another gentleman came forward, saying 'we don't think that is enough, here is a further £1000 from IMPS (The Invicta Military Preservation Society)'.

Rex Cadman then gave me another £1000 on behalf of the War and Peace Show. Even more bewildering, Mr Brent Pollard, owner of the Hop Farm, gave me £1000. It was beyond my wildest dreams, and if all that was not enough, people at the dinner started coming up to me and putting ten and twenty pound notes into my top pocket. Talk about being overwhelmed. I could not speak in case I cried. I do remember that somebody shouted out 'I bet that's the first time Albert has been short of words', and he was right. Anne agreed. The total count was nearly £4000; way more than enough to pay the balance for the Churchill tank that Carl Brown had supplied and restored.

I now had to think about the dedication of the tank, which was no easy task. My first approach was to the Royal Tank Association at Bovington in Dorset, where the Tank Museum is situated. This proved to be the right way to progress. Unfortunately, they wanted full control and I would have to accept what they would do. But me being me, and those who know me will bear me out, that is not the way I work. I will work with people, but I will not be dictated to.. It was at this point that I suggested that we hold a meeting at Bovington to discuss details - just another of my crafty moves. I guessed that the association would try and fill all the seats with their own people, including majors, colonels and the like. I first arranged a meeting with the London branch of the Royal Tank Regiment Association, and at this meeting I explained how I wanted the dedication to proceed. I was hoping for a service, a military band, veterans and their relatives. Also I wanted military representatives present, like The Royal Artillery, Royal Tank Regiment and so on. I required a Padre and a high-ranking military officer to take the salute. Not forgetting, of course, a bugler to play the Last Post and Reveille. I also explained to them that it would appear that the HQ Tank Association wanted to control everything, which I was not prepared to let them do, so I asked them to back me, with three coming to the meeting in support. There were about thirty at that meeting, and all of a sudden a big cheer went up, with one of them saying that this was the opportunity they had been waiting for. They explained that they too were always being told what they can and can't do. They also explained that at the unveiling of a tank memorial in London, it had been decided that all veterans would sit in the back seats, with the front ones going to VIPs, major generals, brigadiers and their wives. They had complained, but nobody listened, so they decided not to attend and held their own service at a later date. They all wanted to come to the meeting with me, but there would too many of them, so I agreed that five could come and support me. I felt that would be enough, as I have always had enough confidence to speak up and press my point in the past. There was absolutely no way I was going to back down.

The meeting took place in Bovington, and as I had anticipated there was a colonel, a major, two captains a regimental sergeant major and six of us. I knew that they thought it was peculiar that I had brought five others with me. The meeting started with the handing out of their agenda on how they thought it should proceed. We all took our time to read it, to inwardly digest their suggestions, and nobody spoke for a while. I then handed out my proposals. To say they were shocked is an understatement. They were dumbfounded that I had the cheek to tell them what I wanted – me, a mere civilian, telling them what to do, God forbid. The major tried to use his rank, and said it is not for you to tell us what to do, then one of the London branch of the RTR Association stood up saying 'that is exactly what HQ has been doing to us all along – to all of our associations – and we're fed up with it. Now we have got Albert who is not afraid to speak up, so I think it would be better to listen to him and if we cannot reach an agreeable settlement it will get into the press.' Well of course, that set the cat amongst the pigeons. The RSM stood up looking like thunder and shouting 'you can't speak to your senior officers like that.' Well it was my turn now. I stood up very quietly, looking through the paperwork. I said nothing for a few moments and then I exploded. With my voice raised as loudly and as firmly as I could, I said to the regimental sergeant major that he was nothing to me, and that he was not an RSM just a Mr, the same as all the gentlemen sitting there next to him. I carried on by telling him that he could not use his bullying attitude on me, because I could shout him down any day. As far as I was concerned, he'd still only got his baby voice, and that I was not one of his recruits now. Everyone sat there open mouthed.

I sat down, and after a short while, I asked calmly if the gentlemen were going to look at my agenda, or should I go away and explain to Colonel John Chamberlain, Commanding Officer of the Wiltshire Yeomanry (Tanks) that he had refused. Someone jumped up asking what Colonel Chamberlain had got do with it? That had really got them thinking. My reply was simply that he was my intermediary between Brigadier Tony Faith, 43rd Wessex Brigade, and myself. The colonel was also a very welcome friend, a benefactor to the tank appeal and a supporter of the 43rd Wessex Association. It was, in fact, Brigadier Faith's idea that I should approach the RTR Association with my proposals, and as Tony had explained, it is after all a memorial to all those tank crews who lost their lives in the Battle of Hill 112. I also wanted a response, as it was only courteous, so that if they weren't interested then we would be on our way home and not waste any more of anyone's time. With that, we got up to walk out. Talk about eating humble pie, they started asking us not to go just yet – perhaps they could discuss our proposals and come to an arrangement. That was fine with me, provided we could talk as equals.

At last, we finally got to my agenda, when the colonel stood up, asking if it was all absolutely necessary, as after all it was not a memorial service. It felt like they had not been listening to anything we had been saying – the five RTR veterans and myself included nearly choked. It took me a while to calm them down, as they had got up to go, saying that that was exactly the attitude that they had been talking about, 'always telling us what to do, instead of asking us what we want'. They were saying 'we're not in the army now, but we were proud to have served our country when in need, and it was our mates who were left behind. It was Albert who put the tank on the hill, not any of you. It has taken fifty-five years after the battle that claimed the lives of so many of our friends – no tank person ever thought about it, and it has taken a Royal Artillery man to do it, damn it. You should all be grateful and ashamed of yourselves and it's now our chance to pay our respects with our own memorial where future generations can come and do likewise.'

In the end they had to concede to my proposals. The band, however, was causing some problems, as it was pointed out to us that all forces bands now had to be paid for, except on Remembrance Day, and they as an association could not afford it. I asked how much it would cost, and they said this would have to be found out, but they promised to come back to me through Colonel Chamberlain. I then dangled another red rag and said 'if the funds couldn't be found then I could always call on the French to supply a band'. A gasp of despair went up. 'Please don't do that,' they said 'it would be very embarrassing to us and the Ministry of Defence.' That suited me, I would have loved to have a go at the Ministry of Defence, for the way they treated our fallen comrades. With that, the meeting ended. The RSM came up to me, apologising for losing his temper, and saying that I had certainly put him in his place, and that they could do with a few more sergeants like me.

News came that the band would cost £2,500, and we would have to find food and accommodation for one night. I knew I could get the food and accommodation via the Cote 112 Association and the French army barracks at Carpique airfield. We'd done it the year before, when the British Logistic Corps. put the tank on the hill, but the money was a different matter. I had to start putting my thinking cap on again and wondered who might be the likely candidate - someone with money? My mind moved to the colonel from London who had already helped with the purchase of the tank. It took me a while to think of a way to make the approach, not easy when you think of the way he had already helped so I phoned Chamberlain and ask if he would come to London with me to meet the colonel so we could thank him in person, as I'd never met him before. Whilst there we could brief him on the preparations for the dedication planned for July the 10th 2000. I thought I might be able to turn the conversation around to talk about the cost of the band and explain to him it that it looked as though we would have to get a French band which might make him think.

The meeting was arranged to be held in his offices in London, and very impressive they were too. He owned a civil engineering and design company and he gave us a very warm welcome. He said 'Albert, you should be very proud of yourself in achieving your goal, from what I have seen and heard you never give up the type of person I admire'. He was certainly going to be amenable. I explained to him about the dedication in July 2000, with details of how it would proceed, and also that the Cote 112 Association was laying on a lunch in my honour for two hundred people, half of which I could choose myself. I hadn't told anybody else about this, so Chamberlain was surprised. I didn't mention the band until the last minute, by saying the unfortunate part is that we'll have to get a French band who will not make any charge, whilst the British RTR band wanted £2,500 which was something I had not allowed for and it was a bit late in the day to start looking around for more donations. Poor old Chamberlain went red in the face with embarrassment; after all he was the Lieutenant Colonel of the Wiltshire Yeomanry (tanks), and this was for a dedication and memorial service to all of those tank crews who had lost their lives. It certainly did the trick. The engineer colonel straight away told me not to worry, and that he would pay for the band. What a relief! As I have said so many times, if you don't ask you won't get.

The time came now to decide who would take the salute of the march past by veterans. I had two ex-generals in mind. However, Chamberlain suggested that we should get someone who was still serving in the tank regiments; by doing this it would help the relationship with the RTR Association which was rather strained because of my aggressive attitude. In the end I agreed that the person should be Brigadier Gatsby, the British Military Attaché to the French government. It was certainly the right decision. On the evening before the dedication and upon the suggestion of the RTR sergeant major, the band held a concert for all the local people and a wonderful display it was, even playing for the children to dance to. Everything went smoothly on the day, with the exception that it poured with rain and we all got wet through.

The reception was excellent, with speeches praising my efforts, and a presentation of a Normandy Plaque, which now hangs in the conservatory. Since then I have made friends with numerous Normandy people including mayors and other dignitaries. One in particular is Gilles Osmond, now president of Cote 112, a real gentleman and friend for life.

I must now go back to Swindon Council and the Mayor. I wrote to the Swindon Evening Newspaper, to ask their readers if anyone remembered the Royal Artillery 112 Field Regiment TA's drill hall on Prospect Hill in the Old Town, as very few of the councillors had heard of it. It was not long before the newspaper was receiving calls and letters from all over the county of Wiltshire, criticizing their councillors for their lack of knowledge. It finished up with Wiltshire councillors writing to me and the paper apologizing. It turned out to be just what I needed when it came to another of my projects later on.

At our annual meeting in 2001, it was decided that the 112 Old Comrades Association would have to close down due to the reduced numbers attending. I agreed to that but my question was what we were going to do about the 'laying up' of the Association's Standard. The normal procedure is that the Standard and Old Comrades are paraded through the town (Swindon) together with a band, military personnel, in this case Royal Artillery from Lark Hill School of Artillery, and other troops. To take the final salute would be the Lord Lieutenant of Wiltshire, the Mayor of Swindon and President of the Old Comrades Association. To my surprise everybody was silent, until the chairman remarked that we could lay up the Standard in the nearby church at any time. I was dumbstruck. I had raised the money for the standard and the OCA had been in existence since 1947, fifty-four years, and now nobody seemed to care. It was as though we had never been through the war together and all of our fallen comrades were being forgotten. That was something I could not live with. Our chairman said that if I wanted to do something, that was up to me but whatever it was, they would support me but there was no money available. After the meeting closed and everybody was having the last drink together, our ex-colonel's son, Peter Gadson, came up me to me and pledged to support whatever I had in mind to the tune of £5000. It looked as though God was on my side yet again. So there was me on my own, but with a backing of £5000; a new challenge which I could not refuse.

The next issue was where to start? Organizing the parade would have to be my first priority. It took me several weeks as I had no knowledge of how these parades were organised. My first thought was to approach the RSM at the School of Artillery and ask for his advice. He suggested I find someone from the Swindon Royal British

Legion; he was sure they would be able to help. He told me to get back to him once I'd done so to see what they could do; perhaps they could help by printing the service leaflets and send men to take part. It did not take long before I had a message from a couple of men who were capable of handling the whole parade and the service, which was such a relief. I could now concentrate on the next stage of the project I had in mind.

It was now mid-May 2002. I was aiming to have the parade and the laying up of our standard on Sunday September 1st, 63 years from the day we were called up. I also wanted to do something on the evening of Saturday 31st August. I had an idea but felt that I should form a committee to include Peter Gadson (who's money I was spending), Wilf Blackwell, Secretary of the OCA, and the two gentlemen who offered to organize the Sunday parade. It would be my first time meeting them. After making contact, a meeting was arranged for the last Saturday of May. We held the meeting in the Goddards Hotel. The first thing on the Agenda was the Sunday Parade. The two organizers seemed to have it all in hand; apparently they had done this sort of thing many times, and appeared to know what they were talking about; this certainly impressed Peter, Wilf and myself. Next up was what I wanted to do on the day before, Saturday 31st August. My idea was to take over the Wyvern Theatre in Swindon. I had already found out that it was available that night and how much it would cost, and also what it would take to organize a military band concert as a tribute to the 43rd Wessex Division and 112 Field Regiment, Royal Artillery. Although Peter Gadson had donated £5,000 towards the cost, I thought it was only right that I should try and raise money in other ways rather than take advantage of his generosity. At Peter's request I was not to inform anyone of his contribution, only to the secretary Wilf Blackwell – of course the other two were wondering how I was going to pay for all this. My answer was that I would take care of it, and that I would get people around Swindon to donate some suitably impressive raffle prizes; a new car, beer and champagne, a hot air balloon ride, dinner for two at a local hotel, and many other things. I had already had promises for all these. The new car was given at cost price, all I needed was the go ahead by the committee, which duly came. I had already got someone to print 10,000 raffle tickets free of charge. Also, the Kent Messenger paper would design and pay for 500 special programmes, for which we would charge £3. The programme would give a record of the Regiment and Division during the war. It turned out to be a very desirable and we sold out; a good little earner. I had also secured a deal that the School of Artillery were to print the service sheets.

It was about this time that I became friends with a Lieutenant Colonel Parker, who lived at Wilton near Salisbury. I'm not sure how it started, but I think he had heard about me placing the tank on the hill and also from a radio broadcast I had put out on BBC Radio Wiltshire in Swindon informing listeners of the upcoming event. I must say the support I got from them and the Swindon Evening Advertiser was fantastic. The news was being put out every week, counting down the time. Lt. Col. Parker was another blessing in disguise; he was well known within the Army. He had, before retirement, been CO in the 43rd Wessex Brigade, Belford Camp in Salisbury. He knew all the important people at the School of Artillery and elsewhere. With the excuse that I was going to Lark Hill, I invited him to meet me there and we had lunch in the sergeant's mess. It was whilst there I told him and the RSM of the coming car raffle and the military band concert in Swindon. This proved to be another good move on my part; they both asked for tickets personally but also for 1000 to sell at the School of Artillery, and Col. Parker wanted 3000, with the promise to write to numerous colonels of other regiments asking them for support. In the end, over eight thousand tickets were sold and when everything was completed and paid for I had used only £3000 of Peter Gadson's £5000. I might mention that the two days were a huge success; we got massive coverage in the local paper, with many people writing to me to tell me that their fathers and uncles had been in the regiment but were sadly not with us anymore. I still have the videotapes of the band concert, the laying up of the Standard and the dedication of the Tank in 2000. It rained all through the service, but nobody left.

As I have mentioned, during the war I was involved in Operation Market Garden. In September 2000, Anne, Annette and I went to

Arnhem and Oosterbeek Cemetery for a service for all of those paras and friends of mine who had lost their lives, such as Curly Rolf and Captain Rose. Whilst we were there, I met lots of schoolchildren who came up to me asking if I had been there during the battle. I explained where I had been and what I had done, and that I was not in the paras but the Royal Artillery, firing from the other side of the Rhine, and that I had not been a front line fighter. Their teacher came up and told them not to bother me; now, I always enjoy talking to the younger generation and telling them my experiences during the war. After all, it's only by them talking to veterans that they will appreciate the sacrifice all these men made for the freedom they have today. I turned to their teacher and said 'you bring them over here to learn and then stop them from asking questions? What sort of history teacher are you? Why waste your time and theirs bringing them here if you try to stop them from learning from people who know what it was all about?' Afterwards, I was sorry for what I had said, and especially for embarrassing him in front of the children. After this, me and the history teacher, Nick Dinsdale at the Lady Hawkins School, became great friends, and remain so to this day. So much so, that for the last twelve years I have been invited every other year to go with the pupils from the school to Normandy as their Veteran guide, the latest time being July 2011.

AUGUST 2011

After reading all of this, you must be aware that my interest has always been to make sure that the younger generations are aware of the sacrifice made by my friends and comrades at arms for the freedom they have today, and it is with that in mind I will carry on to the end.

Although it is in its early stages, it is my hope that by the 70th Anniversary of the landing in Normandy on 6th June 1944, we can plant 112 trees to form an Avenue of Remembrance along the new road leading to Hill112. This is still ongoing and we are hoping, eventually, to plant the 112 trees in the shape of a Maltese Cross on ground opposite to the tank with the statue and the 25 pounder field gun. It has taken longer than we thought to attain the ground from the government. Gilles Osmont President of Cote 112 works tirelessly on this cause.

In 2014/15, I went to Dubai to see my daughter Annette for a Christmas and New Year holiday, where we had a wonderful Christmas dinner and New Year's Eve at The Marriott Hotel. I was dancing in my wheelchair with the staff.

The next day, Annette told me that she had a surprise Christmas present for me; she had booked a drive on the Formula 1 race track in Abu Dabi. She knew that I'd always wanted to do this, after we had watched someone racing around the previous year, but she wasn't sure if was too old or if there was an age limit. She said that if anyone asked I should tell them I was 87, seven years younger. However, nobody asked when we signed in; they were just a little surprised that I was disabled, and the disbelieving driver, Tim, when he had to help me into the car, asked me if I was sure I wanted to do this. 'Of course I do!' I said. 'Let's get on with it!'

I must admit I was so excited that I could not wait. We set off and he asked me how old I was. I looked at him with a great big smile on my face and said I'd tell him once we were over the grid line. Me not answering got him intrigues, and as soon we were on the circuit he insisted I tell him or we would turn back. I knew he could not do that, he would have go to all round the circuit anyway. I told him I was 94 in June, and a Normandy veteran. He nearly went off the track in utter surprise, saying that I was the oldest English person he had ever driven on the circuit, and as far as he knew I was the only Normandy veteran to do it, and that he had never seen one of us in Dubai or Abu Dabi. He obviously reported this to the manager, who in turn told the media, whereby he has offered me a discount for next year, providing I give an interview to the media for publicity to encourage more older people to try it!

In June 2014, I informed the president of Cote 112, Gilles Osmote, that I would like to place a sculpture of an Infantryman on the Hill as a memorial to all infantrymen who fought in the battle for Hill 112. This was the first time I have suggested my own project; all the others have been done at the suggestion of others. The 43rd Wessex, rightly so, had their own monument there, and Cote 112 had placed their own, which gave the 43rd Regiment their positions during the battle, and also stone plinths bearing the numbers of civilians who were killed around the commune from Etterville, Baron, etc. And of course the tank was placed on the hill in 1999 as a memorial to the tank crews who had died during the battle in 1944.

I knew there were other divisions who had fought there besides the 43rd; a total of some 65,000 men including the tank units, so I felt that the other divisions should have their own memorial in the shape of an Infantryman with rifle and bayonet leaning forward as though going into battle. It was agreed by the Cote 112 Association that it could go ahead. This was only an idea at that the time, June 2014.

I started looking around for a sculptor who would be able to make such a statue for me. I found one, but the cost was £30,000 which I knew would take me two or three years to get raise donations for. I spoke to Rex Cadman of the War and Peace Show, who told me that he knew of a sculptor in London who had already made a similar statue to the one that I had described to him. The sculptor's name was Michael Whitely London Ltd. So Rex gave me his phone number, and I duly phoned him. Michael said he would be happy to make a statue, providing I gave him a good image of what I wanted it to look like, which I duly sent him. At the same time I invited him and his family to come over to Normandy in June as Annette and I would be there, and said that if he could make it he should make sure that he booked a hotel now as they are filling up fast due to the 70th anniversary of D-Day landings. Apparently he had already booked and was coming anyway.

I met Michael, his wife and family on the 5th and we went to lunch, together with many others. When Michael walked in to the restaurant he carried what I can only describe as a very large picture. He put it down beside him and we started our meal, but curiosity got the better of me so I asked him what it was that he had brought in with him. When he picked it up, everybody else was busy talking and eating so took no notice. He then showed me; it was a photo of a Spitfire. It was one of three he had made and felt he should show it to me to illustrate what his company could do. I must say I was very impressed, and at the same time Michael asked if I would sign it, which I duly did (one of many over the years). Michael then explained to me that his family had all agreed that the memorial would be made free of charge, and also that he would take it over to Normandy and erect it ready for unveiling on the 12th July 2015. I was completely gobsmacked. I was unable to control myself and shouted 'Michael has given the statue free of charge!'. Everyone stopped eating and looked up with complete surprise before singing 'For he's a jolly good fellow', accompanied by much cheering, whooping and whistling.

In September we were told by Hayley, daughter of Michael Whiteley, to expect a phone call from a Mr Tom Kelly from Ireland, as he wanted to speak to me about an important matter. I explained to Hayley that I didn't know anyone in Ireland unless it is a relative, as I know my father's forbearers originated from Ireland. I only had to wait five minutes before the phone rang. It was Tom Kelly, who turned out to be from a company called Bartlett Trees. He said that he had heard that I wanted to plant 112 trees on Hill 112 in Normandy. I told him that this was indeed my plan, but that it was going to cost me £5000. He told me that Hill 112 was a place he had been to many times, and said he'd heard that I was the one who'd placed the tank on Hill 112, and that this was something he'd always admired. He offered me his congratulations, and then – even better – told me that he'd spoken to the manager at Bartlett Trees, who had agreed that they would donate, plant, stake and tie the trees as and when required. Lady Luck was with me yet again.

It was after I got permission to erect the statue that I made the comment to Gilles that this would be my last project. His reply was 'no, we want a twenty-five pounder gun as a memorial to all of the Royal Artillerymen, and we would like it for July 2015'. This was also in June 2014, which gave just thirteen months to find a gun. This was a tall order and it took me until March 2015 to succeed. In the meantime, I was going to have to find £10,000 to cover the cost of buying a suitable gun; would thirteen months be enough time to raise it? My goodness, was there no end to what people wanted me to do? At least I had the £5000 which had been saved by Bartlett donating the trees. It meant that I only had to find somebody else who would help me. This came when Ben Oostra of Els Kantoore Efficiency, Holland came to the Hill for a service, and immediately offered financial help, a wonderful gesture and a kind man.

12th of July 2015 was the date set for the unveiling of the statue and the 25 pounder. But who was going to unveil them? After much discussion with Annette, Gilles in France and the Association secretary, we felt that the Earl of Wessex would be the ideal person. We were attending the 43rd Wessex 70th anniversary memorial service at Hill 112 in 2014 and Prince Edward had been there as well. Following the ceremony at lunch, I was with a group of school children from the Lady Hawkins School in Herefordshire. I have been a veteran battlefield guide for their history department since meeting them at the memorial service at Oostebeek in Holland (see Appendix 1). As I was busy, Annette went to speak to the prince and tentatively asked him if he would unveil the statue and the twenty-five pounder the following year. He told her immediately that he would be delighted to do it. We had to follow the correct protocol and write a letter to Buckingham Palace for his personal attention; this would ensure that it was an official approach so that he would be able to add it to his schedule the following year. He was also invited by the Cote 112 Association.

The plans had to be organised for the ceremony. We wanted a military padre to conduct the service, who turned out be Mandy Reynolds. There would be local dignitaries and of course veterans both English and French. We invited a Dutch concert band to come and play by the 43rd Wessex memorial. All the plans were dropping into place. We had one major issue, and that was to make sure that both the gun and the statue were in place in good time. This was problematic to say the least.

Annette and I had to go to a meeting to discuss the positioning of both memorials. I knew where I wanted them to be placed and in which orientation. This would be temporary so that they could then be repositioned later to their permanent position. It was finally agreed to set them up in the simpler locations on the lower ground around the tank to allow for photo opportunities and ease of relocation later after the planting of the trees.

The statue and the gun arrived on the 11th, after complications over transport. The two plinth stones were erected but in such a way that they could be moved later. The statue was delicately placed on top and Michael Whitely, the sculptor, added the finishing touch by putting the bayonet onto the end of the infantryman's rifle. Up to this point I had no idea of what to expect, except to say I trusted Michael implicitly. Annette made sure I couldn't see it and only when Michael was ready was I turned around in my wheelchair. My God, it took my breath away and tears of joy streamed down my cheeks. I could not speak, much to the amazement of all around me. The statue was just how I had pictured it in my mind's eye. Michael had obviously interpreted our chats perfectly, and as a result had made a very moving memorial to the PBI, (the poor bloody infantry). At the same time, I also had to reacquaint myself with an old friend; the 25 pounder. This gun had served me well through out the war and I knew every square inch of it. It was good to see this particular example looking brand new.

[*Twenty-five pounder gun at Hill 11*]

The big day arrived and everyone started arriving in good time for the memorial ceremony and unveiling by Prince Edward. The state was covered with fabric, and the gun was draped with a Union flag. The band were seated by the Wessex memorial and the dignitaries were seated along the route of the old road. Some military vehicles arrived and parked behind the statue. The BBC sent a camera crew to film it for TV in the south west. As the clock ticked closer to eleven o'clock, the anticipation grew for the arrival of the prince. Just before eleven, we heard the sound of a helicopter approach and land; a few minutes later he walked past the tank with his entourage and said hello to all the veterans. He had time for everybody. At eleven, everyone took their places and the service began. It was emotionally charged for me as this was the culmination of several decades of hard work to get proper recognition for what the British soldiers did to help liberate this part of France.

Following the official ceremony, Prince Edward had the pleasure of unveiling the statue and tank. He also 'planted' a single tree to represent the 112 trees that will be planted for 2016. Everyone crowded round to have a chat to him whilst he had photographs taken with the veterans, the statue, the sculptor and so on; he was so patient. After the unveiling, we headed down to Esquay, Notre Dame, for lunch where we all had another chance to chat with everyone and catch up whilst having a bite to eat. The Prince and Gilles made speeches thanking everyone for attending. This was very entertaining, as they made their speeches in both French and English. The prince said his goodbyes and off he went in the Royal Flight's helicopter from the tennis courts. What a fabulous occasion it had been. To mark the event, Annette had booked out a restaurant for anyone who wanted to come and have an evening meal and relax after such a busy day. It was the perfect end to a perfect day.

[Statue]

[*Tree of Peace Ceremony*]

I wonder what is in store for me during the coming years? Well, I will keep going as long as the Lord wishes, as my daughter Annette and son Royston have said I am too good and kind to be taken away just yet. Perhaps reaching one hundred would be a good goal to aim for. I look forward to my letter from the Queen. Here's hoping.

Eratum -
Hill 112 The Documentary

It was in May 2001, I had an idea of making a documentary of the Battle of Hill 112, but before this, I had met Martin Jones who was at that time a freelance cameraman working for the BBC and when I told him of what I had in mind about making a documentary of the battle of Hill 112 he was all for it.

Fast forward and my next step was to make contact with MP Bill Cash whose father Paul, was in my Regiment, and was killed at Normandy in 1944. I also spoke with our local MP Julian Brazier and on doing so, they suggested that I should approach the 'Ministry of Defence Veterans Challenge Fund Committee', also Wing Commander Tootal [retired] who then offered his service as he knew nearly everyone at the Challenge Committee.

All of this was arranged in early 2005, with a meeting between myself, Julian Brazier, Bill Cash, Patrick Tootal and the Chairman of the Committee and after this the Chairman had to report the proceedings of the day to the Ministry of Defence before another meeting was agreed on. This resulted in a phone conversation with Patrick Tootal, who acted as our spokesman, it was suggested by the MOD that we should have a company to organise the production of the documentary, Martin Jones who I met previously and had expressed enthusiasm had worked with such a company called 421, and was naturally then keen to get involved.

A following meeting with the film company directors required that 421 should present a report on how they intended to make the documentry, would there be reinactors infantrymen, tanks etc. and how much it will cost. The MOD also insisted that at least 20 veterans from all over the country should be involved. The MOD agreed to fund the veteran interviews to the tune of £20,000 for the interviews, this was carried out and the money was all used up and the interviews were handed over to the Imperial War Museum. When we then asked for permissions to use in the documentary the museum wanted additional fees to use what we had arranged to be paid for so this unfortunately fell at this point with no explanation as to how or why this situation had arisen.

In 2010 Martin decided to make another start on the documentary, and during the last six years, has made good progress insofar that he hopes to have the documentary ready by the end of 2016 if the funding can continue to be found. Martin has established some interest from Channel 5, but they will not put any finance into the project until 50% of the production costs can be found elsewhere.

So my next big 'ask' is if there is anyone reading this book who might be able to help in any way, we would be very grateful and hope to complete this legacy for future generations to see what went on at Hill 112.

For more details and contact information please visit my website at: www.albertfigg.co.uk

Thank you.

APPENDIX 1

Twelve years ago, I took pupils of Lady Hawkins School to attend the sixty third year anniversary of Operation Market Garden. Whilst there we saw a WW2 veteran called Albert Figg lay a wreath on behalf of the 43rd Wessex Division. After the service the pupils rushed up to Mr Figg as he was leaving the Oosterbeek cemetery and started to bombard him with questions.

I went over to the children and told them to leave Albert alone and not bother him unduly. I was then taken aback when Albert told me off. He was right of course, as it is imperative that all children have the opportunity to talk to veterans, who will agree that they were just ordinary men who did extraordinary things.

[*Albert &school children Hill112*]

Albert contacted me shortly afterwards to ask if the headmaster would be interested in him accompanying any school trips that went to France to see the Normandy beaches and battlefields. We kept in contact, and it was agreed that Albert travelling with the pupils would enhance their enjoyment of the trip and make the process of learning history so much more interesting.

Since the first trip Albert has become our battlefield guide, and has become an important part of teaching the history of WW2.

To this day he has remained a very dear friend to all of us.

[*Nick Dinsdale - History teacher Lady Hawkins School Hereford*]

Albert Figg and the students of years 11, 12 and 13 of Marcel Mezen High School in Alencon, France

Albert landed on 24 June 1944. He described his 'gunner's war' and his initial contact with the local population to the students of Marcel Mezen High School.

What kind of welcome did you get from the local population?

Not too good to begin with. People resented us and you could hardly blame them, because a lot of French people had been bombed and killed during the Normandy landings and afterwards.

Some of the farmers were the most hostile because they'd lost nearly all their stock. Not only that but we were stealing from them to improve our diet, which consisted almost entirely of dried and tinned food – powdered milk, dried eggs, biscuits, no bread..

One day we went into a henhouse to steal some eggs and then I milked a cow in one of the fields. I'd just filled my tin mug when the farmer came up yelling and waving something at me that looked like a rifle. All I could here was 'ces sales Anglais' ('ruddy English'). So I ran away. Just as I was about to reach my gun, I fell over and spilt all the milk and broke all the eggs I'd put in my pocket/ I was so angry with the farmer for stopping me from getting a proper breakfast that I grabbed my rifle, took aim and fired a shot in the air. The poor man dropped his 'rifle' (which was actually just a piece of wood, as I saw on my way back from the field) and ran off as fast as he could, convinced I was going to kill him. Now you can see why the farmers weren't too happy.

But hadn't you liberated them?

Of course, and since then I have come to realise just how grateful the people of Normandy are. In fact I'm very keen to thank them on behalf of all the veterans, for the wonderful welcome they gave us every time we come to France, and for the respect they show all our comrades-in-arms who are buried here, by taking good care of all the memorial sites.

I've also noticed that they call us 'heroes' – I've never considered myself to be a hero, we were just soldiers who came to do out duty and liberate you. For me, the true heroes that I will never forget were the members of the Resistance.

The long history of generous hospitality has never been broken, and no-one has ever made the slightest complaint about the losses caused by our bombs or our artillery – for which I was partly responsible. Unfortunately, the instruments of war make no distinction between friend or foe, and that is one of the horrors of war…

Did you kill anyone?

Not that I know of. In fact I have no idea, because I was in charge of a twenty-five pounder gun that was positioned near the rear – I was firing three and a half miles behind the lines. To tell the truth, I never even saw the enemy during the fighting, I only saw the prisoners of war we'd taken once the shooting had stopped.

What effect does not knowing have on you?
No particular effect, because I'd never really thought about it.

How did you feel about the German soldiers?
I've met lots of them, and I've even shaken their hands once or twice – but they were all just ordinary soldiers from the Werhmacht. They were no different from English soldiers; they obeyed orders because if they didn't fight or ran away they were shot. The only Germans I've ever hated were the SS. They systematically committed murderous atrocities, such as they killilling all the members of the Resistance imprisoned in Caen as a reprisal against the Normandy landings. They left the bodies in a courtyard for our troops to bury.

Adrien's Impressions (a student at Alencon College)
'We didn't meet a hero, but 'just a liberator', to quote his own words. Soon enough we were bonding with him. He told us about his war, with many personal details. He also passed the baton to us, saying: 'You must be ready to fight for peace. Remember, people who died so that you could live in peace are no longer with us… So now it's your turn to build and preserve this peace and pass it on to future generations…'. He also told us how lucky we are to live nowadays. He made us understand that in everything, even in war, you have to hold on to the positive. But he was never able to forget the young sixteen year old boy who had enlisted and died in battle, or how his best friend died before his eyes three weeks before the end of the war. He cried and was unable to finish his story. It made us feel so heartbroken to see a veteran cry. Seeing him try to get up from his wheelchair when the British national anthem played also made an impression on us. He has had an incredible life; he went around the world twice and learned to use a computer at age 85. He still has plenty of plans on his mind, even though he is aged 94, he's not old!'

REMEMBRANCE

Remembrance to me, means memories of all those young faces left behind.

As age catches up with us, those words 'They shall not grow old as we who are left grow old' could not be more true.

Also the memories of the first of September 1939, when the Territorials were called up to fight the evils of Nazism. I see my mother standing on the doorstep, crying her eyes out, and wondering if she would ever see her son again. She had two sons and four sons-in-law already in the army, and now her baby was going. I was the youngest out of eleven, and she wondered if she would ever see us again. She had seen the horrors of the first World War; relatives gassed, blind, wounded, and many thousands of men never to return home.

It was many years after, whilst saying goodnight to my mother's photograph, I started to see tears pouring down her face and I wondered how many mothers were doing the same in 1939.

It was at this point I wrote this eulogy.

> **Mother's Sons.**
> My dear son is now eighteen
> He will soon be going
> The dark grey clouds are growing
> which say, the Hun is coming.
>
> The time now comes to say goodbye.
> Mother at the door with tears in her eyes.
> She had seen it all before; many of her friends had made the fall.
>
> Son now trains with his gun,
> In his excitement to meet the Hun.
>
> It's his commitment, in the end,
> to make all bodies see peace again.
> Son now in some foreign land,

Blistering heat, and deep, deep sand.

He has pride in his job
and still going strong with his char & wad,
But that is not much good against the 88,
But is a British Heritage on any date.

Son writes home, at last,
He says the Hun is running fast
And it will not be long
That this war will last.

The time goes by
there is a knock on the door,
Mother turns to Dad, and says I've heard that before

It is dark out there,
I cannot see
But she already knew it was he

Home at last, safe and sound
But away again, I will be bound,
Son has to go finish the task.

But he is not very far away,
as he trains for another day,

It was one hot day,
In June 1944
She heard the news
Of our lads on the shore,
The name of which she is not sure.

The tanks and guns are pouring in
To beat the hun for their great sins
Mother then knelt down, and said a prayer,
Please dear God make him safe
His duty he will do I am sure
But I require him more and more

For should he die, I would too.

Not that I ask for him alone,
Others there, are also mother's sons
So please dear Lord,
Hear my prayer,
So that others know you care

Son writes home at last
News is brief, for this is war on nearby shore,
Poppy fields in sight galore
and there is more and more
Than I have ever seen before.

Mother dear, I remember afore,
Of going to war,
We were young in those early days,
Now I wish it would go away,
The horrors of war leaves a scar,
As we look around, for mates gone afar,
The poppy fields have gone a brighter red,
It is the blood of all those mates,
Mother dear, I have to stop,
The sergeant shouts, it is time to go over the top,

We have a task, we all now fear,
Because the hun is so near,
The tiger tanks surround the hill,
As we advance with little thrill,
The guns roar, machine guns chatter,
How many fall it does not matter,
The battle goes to and fro,
First it is us, and then the foe
Around each day,
Another mothers son doth lay.

Little shelter have we got,
Ripe yellow corn on its stock,

And every move we make,
It shakes its head, as though to say,
Please, don't make me your bed.

We now had reached the top,
A ten-acre plateau is all we've got,
One more effort someone shouts,

The DCLI takes over the fight,
Victory is ours,
Another cries, he is right,
It is in our sight,
The wood in the distance is our goal,
But with many a son lost, it has taken its toll,
Not much cheer for the DCLI
The battle won, but with many tears in their eyes.

A memorial stands on Hill 112,
It is to their lives freely given,
There is another next to this,
It is to liberty which Normandy sorely missed.

To the suffering in those early days,
Which altered their lives in so many ways,
Churches destroyed, schools too,
But many were ready to offer us a brew.

Chocolates for children
Cigarettes for dad
Was their cry
We thought they were mad,
Shells and bullets, they didn't care
They knew that freedom was theirs.

Now their memorial, it doth say
Let us have peace every day.

Now the memorial tank is in its place
Other mothers of sons can say grace

May no sons ever be forgotten in our haste,
As we wonder was it a waste?

Please dear Lord, answer our prayer,
So that we remember them lying out there,
As we know, they were all mother's sons,
With their lives, they gave their all.

WE REMEMBER THEM